THE LIFE AND TIMES OF

CYRUS ALEXANDER

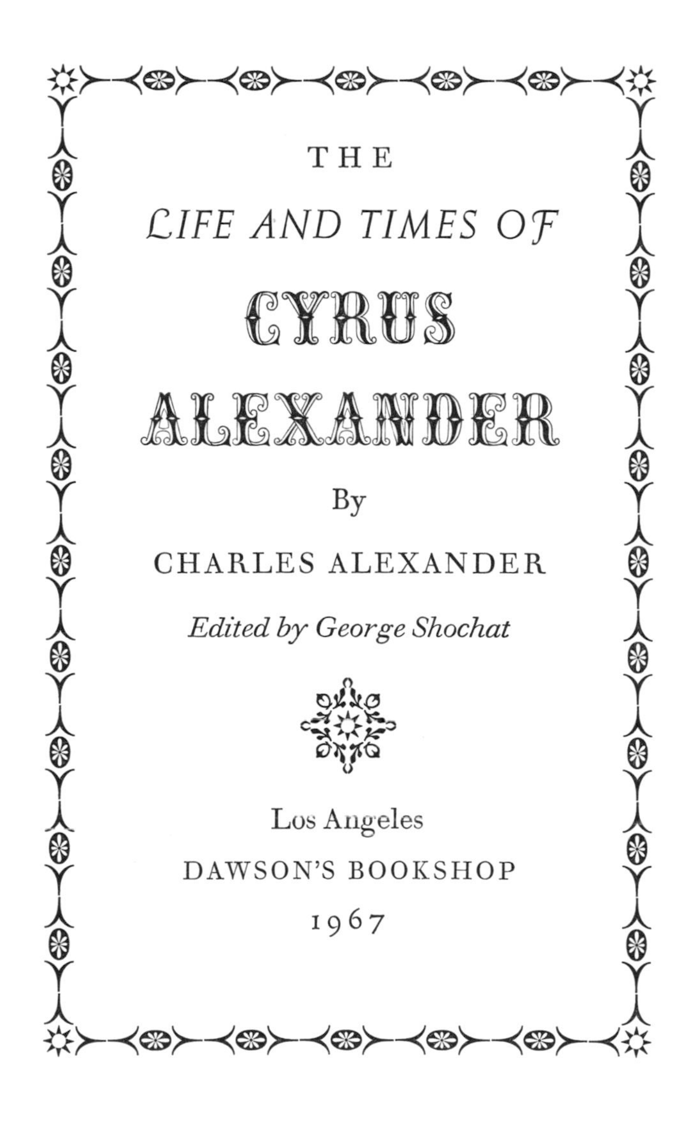

THE

LIFE AND TIMES OF

CYRUS ALEXANDER

By

CHARLES ALEXANDER

Edited by George Shochat

Los Angeles

DAWSON'S BOOKSHOP

1967

350 COPIES PRINTED BY SAUL &
LILLIAN MARKS AT THE PLANTIN PRESS
LOS ANGELES : AUGUST 1967

FOREWORD

THE BANCROFT LIBRARY of the University of California has graciously made available for publication an original manuscript in its collection: *The Life and Times of Cyrus Alexander*, written by Charles Alexander. This biography is another of the fascinating accounts of an early California pioneer, in this case, one of the "mountain men" who went west as a young trapper and, after many vicissitudes, arrived in California well before the great influx which followed the discovery of gold. Starting in Lower California and San Diego in the early 1830's, he settled in what is now the Healdsburg area in Sonoma County.

The present account of an early California pioneer who seems to have been respected and admired as an upstanding citizen by those who knew him, was written by his nephew, Charles Alexander. The circumstances under which the biography was written are explained in detail by the author in his preface. In an effort to preserve the distinctive atmosphere and style of the original, only the most distracting errors of orthography and punctuation have been altered. Yet, despite certain minor inaccuracies and a strong tendency by the author to intrude his personal attitudes and opinions, we are still struck by the rich, adventurous life of Cyrus Alexander, a man who played a significant role in the early days of California before, during and after the Gold Rush.

GEORGE SHOCHAT

Los Angeles, California
June, 1967

CONTENTS

ILLUSTRATIONS

INTRODUCTION*

TO THE GENEROUS PUBLIC. *There are certain classes of books that need no introduction. The titles will show their object. No man writes merely for a passing hour; his book is to be read by unborn generations, and is to become a part of their character and destinies. In presenting this volume to the generous public, I feel confident that they will at least give it a passing look. Had Cyrus Alexander been a general in the army or a president of the United States, or one of our leading Senators, his name would have been heralded throughout our free and glorious country. But because he was simply a farmer, many are ready to pass him by. Alexander was a public benefactor, even if he only occupied the humble walk of life. No one ever went hungry from his door; he was ever ready to help suffering and afflicted humanity. He, from a poor sickly penniless boy*

*Edward H. Kraft, who had come to California from Illinois early in the 1870's, lived for a while with Cyrus Alexander in Alexander Valley. He taught penmanship to the family children. In 1878, he became a partner with the Mulgrews of the Healdsburg *Enterprise*. After leaving the *Enterprise*, he became a school teacher. He never married, and died at his brother's home in Alameda about 1910. (From a letter from Edwin Langhart, Healdsburg City Clerk, August 24, 1965.)

worked his way up to wealth and independence. He was determined to win and he won. His career as a hunter and California pioneer will answer many questions concerning the Golden State. His various incidents of Trappers' life will be read with interest. The book is not fiction but reality. Thousands are turning their eyes towards California. Hundreds of them will be glad to turn back again; they only look at the bright side of things. This work if read closely will give a good idea of California as it was, and as it is to-day, viewed and compared by one who was born and bred in the rich Mississippi Valley.

EDWARD H. KRAFT

Healdsburg Cal.
March 1st 1876.

PREFACE*

IT IS WITH RELUCTANCE that I undertake to write a book, it being altogether out of my line of business. My life so far has been in a different direction. It is not often that a tiller of the soil has leisure time to attend to more writing than his business calls for and a correspondence with his relatives and friends. But feeling that the busy life and various transactions of Cyrus Alexander have been so identical with such an important part of the first history of his adopted state, and that his many friends and others would like to know some of his adventures, transactions, and secrets of success, I have undertaken a work that is so arduous for me to accomplish. I have no letters or notes to begin with, except as memory serves me, and items taken of what has been talked about while

*Charles Alexander came to California from Illinois in 1850. He bought land from his uncle Cyrus, and resided in Alexander Valley for eleven years. In 1861 he went to San Jose and three years later returned to his ranch. In 1880, he moved to Healdsburg, where he later retired. He died there in 1896. His wife was Achsah Smith, daughter of Levi Smith, who located in Alexander Valley in the early 1880's. Mrs. Charles Alexander died in 1894. Five children were born to the Alexanders: Amelia, Josephine, Lawrence, Alice, and Julius. (Edwin Langhart letter cited above.)

in a social capacity around his fire side. I arrived in California in July 1850. And finding my uncle and his family alone, I made arrangements to stop with him for a time. Being without books or papers to read, and having nothing with which to while away our time during the rainy season and long winter evenings, we naturally spoke of things past and gone. He had a thousand questions to ask me about his old home in Illinois, his relatives and friends, and what changes had taken place since he had left home. I answered to the best of my ability, and he in turn would tell me of his adventures in the Rocky Mountains, on the Plains, and the early days of California. I have often since thought that had I noted down more items, this volume might have been a far more interesting book. I lived with him two years and knew him before he left Illinois. We lived quietly, not disturbed by anyone, and perhaps no one enjoyed the confidence he reposed in me; he would relate his troubles to me and tell me of his hopes and fears. Often times, being inquired of for notes of his life and times, I began to pick up items and noted them down for future reference. And now feeling that I am the only one that enjoyed his entire confidence, and having had more conversation with him than with any other person, I feel in honor bound–perhaps it is my duty–to lay the facts before the public. Hence the appearance of the book entitled: "*The Life and Times of Cyrus Alexander*." The book contains the facts just as they occurred. Hoping that they will be of some benefit to my young readers and that it will furnish a history of California, particularly Sonoma County and the country, climate, soil, and farming community around San Francisco, and that many may be profited by watching the energy, integrity and perseverance of Cyrus Alexander, I respectfully submit this volume for your inspection, criticism and perusal.

CHARLES ALEXANDER

THE LIFE AND TIMES OF
CYRUS ALEXANDER

CHAPTER I.

Early Life of Cyrus Alexander

CYRUS ALEXANDER, one of the early pioneers of California, was born in Pennsylvania on the 5th of May 1805. His father, David Alexander, moved from Pennsylvania to the Territory of Illinois in 1810, and settled in what is now called St. Clair County, about six miles from Belleville, the County-seat, and sixteen miles from St. Louis, Missouri, which was then a French trading post. His family consisted of eight children, six sons and two daughters. Cyrus was next to the youngest of the children. Mr. Alexander began life as a farmer, and [went] with others to "open up" the rich Territory of the so called "Far West."

Our hero in his boyhood had very poor health, never being very stout or robust, and consequently not fitted for the rough and tumble farm life of early times. He spent the most of his [boyhood] in reading such books as could then be obtained. Books were scarce and schools almost unknown. His favorite books seemed to be books of travel, Lives of Pioneers, Explorers, Discoverers, Adventurers, Hunters etc.

In disposition, Cyrus Alexander was quiet and reserved, never having much to say, and keeping most of his thoughts and plans to himself. He possessed pluck and determination, and was somewhat solitary in his ways, but was nevertheless a general favorite among his early associates.

He was truthful, temperate and always put all his energy into his work. If misfortune baffled him, he bore his troubles with Christian fortitude and pressed on with renewed vigor. He knew no such word as fail. He was in no ways addicted to the many vices which lead young men astray. Characteristically the rising generation will do well to follow his example.

His parents, hoping that he would outgrow his infirmities if shielded from hard manual labor, encouraged him in his favorite pastime of reading. By this means he early acquired a desire of leading a roving life of travel and adventure. His mind was thus early made up to lead a roving life, and nothing seemed to cause him to change his mind. I might add that this disposition of his became a second nature to him.

His parents, however, like many more of the early settlers of the West, although possessing the necessaries of life, could not afford any luxuries, and were therefore unable to aid their boy in carrying out his boyhood ambition and childhood dreams. He therefore was compelled to help at home, to work and wait, and watch his chance, until he would be able to strike out for himself.

About this time his brother William learned the tanner's trade, as this was then considered a paying business. Cyrus turned his attention to tanning, and assisted his brother until he also understood the business. In connection with this he learned to make shoes and became quite an expert at the business.

His brother Hugh owned and ran a small tread power flouring mill. Here we next find Cyrus at work; he worked with his brother Hugh until he learned the milling business; the principal points considered were how to gear and ungear the machinery, how to dress the mill-stones, and the management of a mill in general. Both of these trades are mentioned here to show his determination and willingness to take hold of anything that came along, and because they proved of great value to him in after life.

His first tramp was made in 1827, he then being twenty-two years of age. In this year the "Lead Excitement" broke out at Galena, Illinois. Rumors were afloat of the wonderful discoveries of rich lead mines, rich strikes, and the fortunes to be made in a short time. As these rumors agreed with his boyhood dreams, he concluded to try his luck at lead mining.

His reasons for going were obvious: first for the benefit of his health; second to see how actual travel and camp life would agree with his early ambition; third, the most important of all, to make his fortune, to get rich. After collecting and disposing of his property and stock on hand, he invested all in an outfit consisting of four yoke of oxen, a heavy and substantial wagon, necessary mining tools, and provisions for the journey.

After all was ready, he bade his friends goodbye, and started on his long journey of four hundred miles for the Galena Lead Mines on Fever River in the northern part of Illinois. As he felt sure of making his fortune, and Illinois being almost one continual sheet of prairie yielding abundant grass for his team, he pressed on his way cheerfully, never stopping to murmur, or once thinking of turning back.

It is perhaps needless to add that many of his friends tried to persuade him to stay, for those who knew him knew him well enough to know that if he once made up his mind to go, that he would go in spite of all they could say or do. Arriving at his destination he went to work like a [man] that meant business. He worked hard and faithfully for several months, but soon found out to his sorrow that his fortune did not lay in lead mining.

Besides this, the rigorous climate and the raw winds of the "Prairie State" did not agree with his delicate constitution. As success did not crown him here, he concluded to go home, his health a little improved by travel, and financially about the same, as he did not gain or lose much by the operation. We will say that he rather gained, as he tested and enjoyed camp life. He now began to retrace his steps over a trackless prairie, very sparsely settled, and concluded to try his hand at something more lucrative.

The next thing that attracted the attention of Cyrus was the Fur Trade that was carried on between St. Louis and the "Far West," the North Pass of the Rocky Mountains, and the Territory of Oregon.

As he was watching every opportunity for a chance of bettering his condition, he was greatly interested in everything he could read and hear of the Fur Trade. He concluded to risk his chances and try his luck in this enterprise. His friends again [tried to prevail] on him to give up his hazardous undertaking. They told him of the horrible Indian massacres, scalping, the danger of wild animals, starvation, privation, of the many chances of freezing to death in the bitter cold climate of the Rocky Mountains, and the poor show of a fortune in such a dangerous and perilous undertaking.

But his determination again carried the day, and strange as this may seem to many of my readers, these terrible obstacles only seemed to increase his zeal to go. He therefore now began his preparations for this his *great* and for aught he knew his *last* undertaking. He now sold his oxen and wagon, and began purchasing a new and different outfit. His first purchase was a horse, an animal well known throughout the neighborhood for his many good qualities, and strength and endurance. He next bought a mule for a pack animal, the very essential traps, and last, but by no means of the least importance, a gun.

The last named article is the best friend a man in Cyrus' occupation can have, as it will be true when all others have forsaken him. A friend of Cyrus' who went by the name of Uncle Sam, dubbed so on account of his many noble qualities, owned just such a gun as our hero wanted to possess. Uncle Sam was a good hunter, a crack shot, and his rifle was acknowledged the best in the country. He never failed to bag his game if once within range of his trusty rifle, and he had many times refused to sell it at high prices. Cyrus made up his mind to own this gun; he therefore went to see Uncle Sam about the gun.

He told Uncle Sam his plans and stated that he wanted the gun, and hoped he would oblige him by selling him the gun. Uncle Sam replied thus—"Wall, Cyrus, I have refused to sell my gun time and again, because it is a good un, and I can't hardly git along without it. But see-in its you and you must-nt go off there without a good gun I rather guess I'll have to let you have it." So the price was agreed upon, and our hero had the honor of owning the best gun in the country. We will see what good use he made of it.

His next purchase was also an indispensable article. It was a brace of pistols of the percussion cap style; these were a great curiosity as they were the first of the kind seen in his neighborhood. While his traps were being made, he had leisure time to visit his friends and exhibit the "elephant." Various conjectures were made about the new patent pistols, and our hero was considered the "lion" of the day.

The next step was a matter of very important consideration. Should he go as an employee in the Sublette Fur Company then forming at St. Louis or should he volunteer as an independent under their protection? He concluded to go as an independent as it gave him more latitude; he could thus be his own "boss," and if fortune suited he would have a better show for the lion's share.

All being ready in the spring of 1831, he started on his perilous expedition for the Rocky Mountains as a trapper, fortune seeker, explorer, discoverer, and as one who is not satisfied unless on the tramp.

Reader, just picture to yourself the parting between Cyrus Alexander and his praying mother, his much loved and respected sisters and brothers (his father being dead). None knew if they should ever have the pleasure of meeting again upon earth. Cyrus little dreamed that this was the last time he should ever be embraced by his mother, and receive her kind instructions for his future welfare. Everything must have an end and so had the parting of Cyrus from his relatives and friends.

He now turned his face westward, to enter an unexplored wilderness, surrounded by every danger imaginable, and entire strangers for associates; no mother to soothe, no sister to caress, or brother to encourage him in his struggles and triumphs of his chosen vocation. You may wonder if he ever hesitated. No, he was determined to go; he had made up his mind to go, and go he would, let come what will.

When he crossed the Mississippi River and stood on the western bank of that noble stream, he cast one more longing farewell look upon his adopted state, just across the stream; he also cast a farewell look upon the Mississippi River. Little did he think at the time that it would be the last time he would ever see the sun shine on that beautiful stream, the pride and glory of this our proud United States. We suppose his manly heart must have beat faster when he turned on his heel, to leave the stream that separated him from all that he held dear. It could not have been otherwise.

He now mingled with others of similar resolutions and occupations, and registered his name as Cyrus Alexander of St. Clair County, Illinois. He and his comrades soon became acquainted; on expeditions like this "the boys" do not stand on much ceremony. If a person is unfortunate to have a long name it is soon shortened, a suffix or a prefix taken off, or a new nickname is introduced. Our hero soon went by the name of "Aleck." He succeeded in getting into the good graces of "the boys," and soon became a general favorite among them.

CHAPTER II.

The Start for the Platte River

AFTER leaving St. Louis, Aleck made arrangements with the Sublette Fur Co. to purchase his furs and to furnish him with ammunition. The company followed up the Missouri River heading towards the Platte River Country, and from thence towards the mountains, constantly on the lookout for passes through which they could take their wagons. They had success with their teams and made good time in coming through the Platte River Country.

Aleck now with two of his companions – White Cotton and Black Harris – separated from the big company, and started towards the Wind River chain of mountains, following up the Yellowstone River. The large company made Santa Fe their head-quarters, and the mountains and surrounding country their fields of labor. Aleck and his companions went higher up into the mountains in quest of Pine Martens, the large Otter, and the numerous Beavers which inhabit this cold and dreary region.

They were quite successful in finding fur bearing animals, but at the same time they were exposed to the mercies of the relentless Crow and Black Feet Indians who claimed this whole region of country. It was also far away from market and communication. After a successful season of hunting and trapping, they gathered up a large number of pelts, and were about to start to market with them, when lo! the "Pesky"–as Aleck called them–Black Feet made a raid on them, robbing them of every pelt. But this was not all; they themselves were handled pretty roughly–that is, handled Indian style; none but the *Noble red skins* know how to torture a *pale face*. They were now tried by an Indian jury. Aleck now began to open his eyes; he soon saw that he had Indians, not civilized white men to deal with; he did not know how near his sands of life were run. Perhaps his childhood dreams were about to end; he now thought of his home, his friends, and their advice. But it was his choice to lead this kind of a life and he had to make the best of it.

He did not know how soon he would feel the edge of the scalping knife he had read and heard so much about; it was no romance now, but stern reality. The Black Feet, however, after holding a solemn council, concluded to let them go this time. The Indians took everything they had excepting their traps and guns;

they left these as they did not know how to set the traps or handle the percussion cap guns, and perhaps thinking they could make another raid and take these whenever they wanted them.

The party was greatly relieved both in wealth and mind, but were very glad to see the Indians take their departure. The sun seemed to shine brighter after their Red brothers had left. They now took their guns and picked up their traps and started in new again, but as winter was approaching and they had lost one year's work, they concluded to go into winter quarters. Their object now was to find a place where they would not freeze or starve to death. They concluded to find as comfortable a place as possible; they succeeded in finding a snug little valley that had the appearance of being a resort for buffaloes, and seemed to be sheltered from the deep snow that fell in the Wind River mountain system. Here they erected a rude cabin and spent their first winter away from home quite independently.

The buffaloes came to this retreat in great numbers and did not seem to take notice of the rude hut. So you [see] they were enabled to select and shoot the best in the drove from their cabin door. They lived almost entirely on beef, and passed the long dreary months of winter as "monarchs of all they surveyed."

As the warm Spring sun began to melt the snow, the buffaloes gradually left. The party now "pulled up stakes," and started for the mountains again, as full of hope as they were at the out-start, nothing daunted at their misfortune of the past year; they had experience now; if nothing else was gained by their past year's work, the Black Feet had taught them at least one dear lesson.

On this trip as on the previous one they depended entirely on their rifles for their sustenance. One day as Aleck and Harris went out on a hunt they left White Cotton to keep camp. Imagine their feeling when on their return they found their companion murdered. Cotton was busily engaged in dressing a skin when a skulking Indian slipped up on him and shot him through the lungs. He evidently fell dead in his tracks, as no signs of a struggle were to be seen. The untimely and sudden death of Cotton cast a gloom over the two surviving men. He had been tried and found faithful and brave; he was a dear and necessary friend to them; their party was small, and they could not think of sparing any of their number. But, "what can't be cured must be endured."

When away from home, relatives and friends, and out in the wilds, among treacherous Indians and wild animals, the ties of friendship seem to be allied more closely than on other occasions. Aleck and Harris buried their dead companion in the mountains, hundreds of miles from his home and civilization, and shed earnest and heartfelt tears over his grave. They left the grave sad and lonely men. They now knew "that a friend in need is a friend indeed."

As Aleck and Harris were now alone and their company too small to carry on business, they concluded to pick up their traps and hunt the large company. Here was another weary march for miles, over a wild country, and no telling how they would fare, or when or where they would find the large company. They started in a southernly direction in the hopes of meeting their old companions at the trading post of Santa Fe.

For once Providence favored them; they found plenty of game on their way, and succeeded in killing several large and fat bears, and saved some bear's grease to celebrate the feast, should they be lucky enough to find the "boys." They found the company stationed near Santa Fe, and you can safely vouch it was a joyful meeting for all of them. The first question was—Where is White Cotton? On informing them of the unfortunate trapper's fate, a feeling of sadness passed over the camp. Cotton was a noble hearted man, a crack shot, and liked by all the "boys." And they all knew that he would be missed, and that his place could not easily be filled.

Aleck informed the company that he would try again if any one would volunteer to fill Cotton's place. A man by the name of Smith offered his services.[1] They now procured some flour from the large company, and made preparations to have a feast on bread shortened

[1] Thomas Long Smith (1801-1866) became a legendary character during his life-time. Robert Glass Cleland (*This Reckless Breed of Men*, p. 272) calls him "the most notorious of the horse-stealing mountain men, according to popular account."

with bear grease. But after one or two trials they gave up the bread question as a poor job. In the first place it was too much trouble to carry the flour with them. In the second place, they had lived on flesh so much that their habits were carnivorous. Their style of cooking meat was quick and simple; they always roasted it mountaineer style, and they enjoyed and relished their frugal meals more than if they had been cooked by a high-toned Negro cook at a first class hotel or restaurant on Fourth Street.

Aleck had now gained one of his long hoped for anticipations, that is, his health. Mountaineering agreed with him; he was now a stout, healthy, robust man; this alone paid for all his trials and privations; he now for the first time knew what it was to be a well man. After laying in a supply of ammunition at the trading post, they set out again to see if fickle Dame Fortune would not smile on them this time.

Black Harris was appointed captain this time, thinking that a change in leaders would bring a change in luck. They now penetrated farther than ever into the mountains, following up the streams, and around the ponds and marshes that abound in that section of the country. Game seemed abundant; they found plenty of beavers, and began trapping immediately, keeping it up as they traveled, sometimes with good success, and at other times finding a "dry haul" as it is termed, when they draw an empty trap. But as they proceeded on their journey, their luck suddenly changed.

As game had been very abundant, they neglected to carry any provisions with them. They now came to a region where game was very scarce. Starvation now stared them in the face. An incident now occurred that may appear laughable to some, shocking to others, and perhaps some will pity, or at least sympathize with the brave but unfortunate "boys," who suffered so much by the operation.

They were on one of their long tramps from one hunting ground to the other, and finding no game, the word was–"boys, we must make a raise pretty soon, or the thing will be up with us." After looking around in vain they suddenly came upon a large swamp; they concluded they might possibly find something here that would satisfy their hunger. They were getting desperate now, and had to force things, not being particular what kind of game they would scare up. After beating about the swamp for some time, they discovered something that looked like a nest in an old stump. And looking more sharply– men are apt to look sharp when they are starving–they saw the head of a goose protruding above the nest.

Aleck was appointed to fire the all-important shot. Roasted goose now danced before his vision, so crawling up as closely as he dared, he took aim and "whanged away," but horror upon horrors, he had counted on his goose too soon. In his nervous and weak condition, and the excitement of the moment, he overshot his mark, and the goose flew away in safety. Perhaps his hunger caused his imagination to wander or made his eye dim, but be that as it may, there was no goose to roast for the starving trappers. Aleck now concluded to take a peep in the nest, so climbing up he peeped in and found it full of eggs; this was some consolation at least. The "boys" got out the frying pan, and putting in some bear's grease, made preparations for the long-wished-for meal.

Imagine their surprise when on breaking the first egg, they found its contents just ready to make its debut; in they went however, bones, feathers and all. Gentle reader, do not let this unnerve you; remember they were starving, and a craving appetite at such times knows no bounds. They fried the goslings hard and brown, like fish. Aleck in telling this said it was the best dish he ever ate; he had often eaten what was pronounced recherche dinners and suppers, but never a meal he had relished one-half so much as this his meal of goslings.

The next day they succeeded in trapping a beaver, which satisfied their hunger for that time. It is really surprising with what apparent unconcern an old trapper will relate circumstances like these; they seem to consider them as a matter of course. Aleck in relating the gosling affair smacked his lips to give us an idea how they were relished.

It would undoubtedly be interesting to my juvenile readers to go on with the "boys" and their many interesting adventures; the ups and downs, smiles and

Alexander Residence, Mendocino Township, Sonoma County

Cyrus Alexander

frowns, their many hair breadth's escapes, exposures to the merciless Indians, their sufferings from cold, hunger and fatigue, their many many tramps; but we do not wish to weary our reader, or to make this one hunting expedition monotonous.

All will readily understand that these furs were intended for the Eastern markets; little do many of the fair sex who sport costly furs think of the hard times the poor trappers have in killing the animals and collecting the furs. As a general rule the more valuable the fur is, the harder the said fur-bearing animal is to capture, many of them having their abodes where it is almost impossible for men to find them. Others again are very shy and hard to approach; besides this they must be captured during the cold and dreary winter months.

As this hunt is getting quite lengthy, suffice it to say that they had a successful hunt and collected quite a number of pelts ready for market when they were again attacked by their ever watchful foe, the Black Feet Indians. The trappers resisted and determined to whip out the Indians. But the majority generally rules, and they did so in this case. The Indians had kept an eye on all their movements, and robbed them of all their furs and pelts, again leaving them keep their traps and firearms.

They now held a consultation; should they continue trapping, or give it up as a poor business and go home and lead a different life? In summing up all they came to this conclusion: they had lost everything they had captured in hunting; whenever their hopes had been raised and hunting had paid well, the Indians had robbed them, but then they were young, active, hale, and hearty; their health had been very good; so they concluded they would try their luck once more, hit or miss.

They now concluded to hunt up the large company once more, so they started for Santa Fe. They were now in a precarious condition, no provision and the ammunition so near all [gone] that each had but one charge for his rifle, three charges only between them and starvation. It certainly would not do to waste a shot now; besides game was very scarce on this route.

They soon had to face starvation again. Ammunition was scarce, and their hunger soon knew no bounds; in crossing a stream, they watched closely to see if by chance some animal would come to the stream to get a drink. While watching the stream an old partly decayed deer came floating down the stream. They tackled the deer and drug him on shore, and judging by the smell he must have been defunct for some time. They however hoped that roasting the meat would take away the putrid smell, so they roasted some of the meat. But it was too much for poor Aleck; his stomach revolted. The other two ate a small piece of meat, and also gave it up. They concluded not to take any mulled venison in theirs. It surely was enough to turn the stomach of any human being. As the venison did not satisfy their hunger, they had to scare up something else.

Smith owned a dog that had followed them in all their wanderings the last year, and all were greatly attached to old Watch; they treated him the same as a human being. They now decided that if no game turned up the next day, they would have to kill the dog. The morrow came by no food, so poor Watch was sacrificed; they threw him on a burning pile of brush to singe off the hair; they could not afford to skin him, as they had to save all of the poor dog they could, and they had no more dogs to kill. Watch kept them alive and furnished food for several days, and when the dog meat was about to give out, they were lucky enough to run across an old mule that was in a pretty fair condition; they killed the poor hybrid, and changed their diet from canine to mule meat, which kept them in provision until they found the large company, somewhere in the mountains west of Santa Fe.

It was customary for the large company to keep a keg of liquor to use on rare occasions, as when they met with old friends, or when they had past common good luck in hunting. On this occasion they concluded to have a big and jovial time. The mug was passed around quite freely, and soon began to have its effect on the "boys"; they had a gay old time; when one of the boys, who was pretty drunk began to show off his agility—if any thing ever will make a fool of man, whiskey surely will—in one of his tantrums, he seized a rifle and fired it off at random. It proved an unfortunate shot for Smith, as it took effect in his knee, thus laying him up in a mountain camp, and no one to nurse or care for him, not even a physician to extract the ball. He suffered untold misery; his leg got worse and worse, until mortification set in, and the poor fellow found that his leg must come off. He begged of his companions to amputate the limb for him; they were determined men ready to do anything, but this was too much for them; they did not have nerve enough to undertake such a surgical operation. So Smith, to get out of his misery began the amputation himself; after his comrades saw that he was determined to have it taken off, they pitched in and helped him with such rude implements as they had in camp. This was one feature they had not counted on, and they were not prepared in instruments or nerve.[2]

In spite of this rough treatment Smith recovered, but had to change his vocation, as a one-legged man would never do for a mountaineer. Years after this we met Smith at Weavertown in California north of Sacramento City; he was stamping around on a wooden leg. After his misfortune he was ever known as Pegleg Smith. We are sorry to add that he turned out a "bad egg."

[2] This is one of many versions of the famous operation. According to Sardis W. Templeton's biography of Pegleg Smith (*The Lame Captain*), the accident and amputation took place in 1827. Variations of both incidents are dealt with in Chapter 2, "With his own knife." All of them differ substantially from the present account.

He married an Indian squaw; perhaps we had better not use that divine word married, as *cahoot* would convey my meaning better. At any rate he used neither minister, license or priest. No wedding cake was used, and brides-maids and grooms-men were dispensed with. He lived in *cahoot* with this squaw for some time in the mountains, but we are sorry to say that he afterwards cruelly deserted his dusky and by far better half, and came down into Sacramento Valley. He was afterwards seen in Napa Valley, and still later than this he came to Alexander Valley, and called on his old trapping companion Aleck.

Aleck and Harris soon found a substitute for Smith at Santa Fe, and concluded that this would be their last hunt; if they met with poor success again, they would return home. Aleck still had some pluck left. But where would they go this time? It was folly to go in the hunting ground of the Black Feet; they had tried this twice to their sorrow, as the reader is aware of; they must also find a place where game is plenty. They concluded to try the tributaries of the Green River and hunt on the divide between the Green and Yellowstone Rivers, in what is now called the United States Park, in the northwestern part of what is now Wyoming Territory.

Aleck gives many interesting accounts of this beautiful and picturesque country, of the beautiful sceneries, natural curiosities, cataracts, timber, lakes, hot springs, etc. Mr. Alexander spent many pleasant days in this region, studying nature in her various forms; he was troubled by no one and had no fears. A large portion of the country in this vicinity is included in the Great Desert. The reader must bear in mind that the "boys" followed the streams and belts of timber, and therefore saw only the better portions of the country. Alkali streams are quite numerous, and the late report of the discovery of gold in the Black Hills part of Aleck's old stamping ground is calling thousands of fortune seekers into this very region.

The writer himself left his loved and sacred home with the expectation of finding his fortune here. But Uncle Sam's blue coats interfered. They are here to guard the Cheyenne Indian Reservation and to keep white intruders out. They are on duty; you can find them playing cards in the saloons in the towns along the great Pacific R. R. So we, like thousands more, came on to the Golden State of California. The G[reat] W[estern] P[acific] R. R. now passes near this country through Cheyenne City. Of the thousands of passengers who now come flying through here on the Iron-horse, but few stop to think of the danger and privations the early hunters and those bound for California had here in early days.

Since we have mentioned the Black Hills, allow me to add that my advice is, for all who can make an honest living at home, never to venture to go to the Black Hills. There is gold there, undoubtedly, but it will require capital to mine and collect it. More money has been sunk in the Black Hills than will ever come out of them.

Thousands of young men are dissatisfied and will not rest until they have satisfied themselves "that Rome was not built in a day." The old saying that "Experience teaches a dear school and fools will learn in no other" is a good one. Now and then a person makes a fortune in the mines, but where there is one successful one, there are ninety and nine who "go below the ford."

Should any of my readers wish to try their luck in the Black Hills, let them bear in mind that they will have many hardships to endure. They will find a country where even sage brush will not grow in many parts of it. The gold is mostly Placer-diggins, and much of it is what is commonly called shot gold.

But we must now follow Aleck in the last named hunt. The boys again saw both sides of life; sometimes starvation was near, and at other times having plenty and some to spare. One morning while in camp and almost out of grub, they discovered two very large bears apparently asleep and enjoying the warm sun on the sunny side of a hill. As the bears were some distance apart, it was an easy matter to arrange how to attack them both at the same time. One was to take the bear to the left, the other the bear to the right, and both to fire at the same time, Aleck to give the signal. After firing, Aleck's bear never moved; the other bear jumped, tumbled, rolled and bellowed at a fearful rate, but finally expired. They were now sure of one bear at least, and concluded they would now approach the one at which Aleck had shot. They advanced very cautiously, loading their pieces on the way; on coming near the "old chap," they found him dead. He had not moved a muscle; the ball must have passed through his heart while the huge animal was drawing a breath. They now had plenty of meat and took a rest to gain new strength for their next tramp.

You thus see that when the trappers had plenty they knew how to appreciate it. Shortly after this as the little party were out reconnoitering, they suddenly came upon the large party. They had a big time as before, but did not fool with the rifles this time. The furs they had were not enough to make it profitable, but they came in very handy in exchange for ammunition. This was on the first day of July, and they concluded to take a rest, have a big chat, and celebrate the 4th in the old fashioned style before again separating.

They were now among the mountains surrounding the Sweet Water River, and finding a large abrupt precipice they ascended the rock, and unfurled the Stars and Stripes and let Freedom's banner flutter to the breeze. The large company carried our country's flag with them, and unfurled it on many a mountain top. The large rock on which they held their celebration, they named Independence Rock, a name which still clings to it, and always will. Many a hunter and California pioneer afterwards used Independence Rock as a land mark.[3]

Perhaps some of my readers think that the boys would forget the 4th of July and home customs, but on the contrary they were just beginning to find out how large this glorious country is. They found many mountains, rivers, valleys, that they had never heard or dreamed about. The rivers here of course were not so large as the Mississippi and Missouri, but then they had a rapid and very strong current, which made them very difficult to cross. In many of these rivers the water does not flow, but leaps and tumbles, and foams at a fearful rate. After the celebration was over and the boys began to get sober, they again separated, Aleck's division striking out for the head waters of the Green River.

Many an immigrant of 1875 will remember the Green River in the spring of that year when the high waters took the U. P. R. R. bridges, also the number of times the Iron Horse crosses this swift current river. The Green River country proved a good hunting ground for the "boys"; here they found beavers in

[3] Independence Rock, in eastern Wyoming, between Fort Laramie and South Pass. Julia C. Altrocchi, in *The Old California Trail*, p. 197, writes: "Far back in 1810 or 1811, Stuart and Crooks and Astor's other adventurers on their way towards their discovery of South Pass, had paused at Independence Rock on the Fourth of July and had given the place its permanent patriotic name." According to John C. Fremont (*Narrative of Exploration and Adventure*, p. 180), "Independence Rock was the most celebrated landmark on the Oregon Trail. So named because some trappers had celebrated the Fourth of July there in or about 1825, it is a huge outcropping of granite . . . about 838 miles from Kansas City by the trail."

abundance, and stopped for a considerable length of time, longer than at any other trapping ground. We will give you a short history of beaver trapping.

This animal, whose fur is so valuable, is unlike all other fur-bearing animals in its habits. Their head-quarters are on streams, where they construct a dam, and then build their huts on the dam, thus forming quite a village. The beaver is a wide awake fellow, never found napping, and much caution and trickery is resorted to in order to capture him. Their dams are so constructed that the water will overflow them the entire length of the dam. They cut the most of the timber some distance above the dam, and float it down the stream to the dam. The teeth in the lower jaw of the beaver are arranged in such a manner as to give him a great advantage as a chopper; the two teeth are long and concave, sharpened in such a manner, that use and wear only seems to strengthen and sharpen them. They move their lower jaw with a jerk, and are enabled in this manner to cut out large chips.

In habit the beaver is industrious and peaceable, hundreds of them living on the same dam. It had been observed that when a break occurs in the dam, all the beavers will go to work at the breach, some cutting timber, others floating, carrying and arranging the timber, still others using their tails as trowels, putting on the mud until the mischief was repaired, when all would return to their huts. Their huts are arranged so that the entrance is under the water, and on entering the huts they dive under the water and then ascend into the hut. The trapper, when all is ready, takes advantage of this peculiarity; he makes a break in the dam, sets his traps, and then quietly retreats for a short time. The beavers, on discovering the break, immediately go to work to mend the dam; while engaged in this they step into the traps.

The hunter returns, takes out his "catch," resets the traps and retires as before; in this way a whole colony may be captured. Aleck and his companions trapped for championship; this made it a little more exciting, but as the beavers were so numerous all of them had success. The water was very cold, and beaver trapping requires a great deal of wading. They remained here until winter set in, and bade them move. This was the best hunting ground they had ever found. Each had what he considered a thousand dollars' worth of furs.

Aleck now considered himself rich; if he could only get his pelts to market, he would start for his home in Illinois. A $1000 in those days would make him quite a prominent land-holder. They now packed up their things and started to meet the large company, but being heavily loaded the large company gained on them so fast that they were compelled to change their route. They knew it would be folly to meet their foe the Black Feet. So they followed down the Green River to the Colorado, thence down the Colorado, towards the Gulf of California. Here the other company had a Fort.

On arriving at the Fort the Indians informed them that the large company had started for Santa Fe. They now concluded to hurry up and follow, so they decided to cross the upper part of the Gulf. The Indians told them it was a dangerous undertaking, but what was danger to them? The Indians at the Fort owned a large canoe which they cheerfully offered to loan them, also to furnish them men to help to row across the Gulf. They packed their guns, furs and traps into the canoe, and bright and early one morning pushed from shore, three Indians accompanying them to help row and to bring back the canoes.

The water was calm but cold; they moved along quietly for some distance, when suddenly a heavy storm of wind and snow arose; the waves ran high and the Gulf became quite rough. They now saw that it was impossible to cross that day, and to their dismay discovered that their canoe was too heavily freighted. They now thought they would turn their canoe and return to shore; in trying to turn the canoe it capsized and dumped them all into the cold water, where the snow was floating. All the heavy articles, as guns, traps etc., went to the bottom and the pelts and furs floated down stream. Three of the crew, one white man and two of the Indians, being good swimmers struck out for the shore; this was the last seen or heard of them.

Aleck with his remaining companions and one of the Indians clung to the bottom of the upturned boat.

Sympathizing reader, just imagine our hero's condition in the freezing water, in sight of land without hopes of ever again putting his foot upon it. The Indians on shore saw them, but had no canoe, and could render no assistance—"but as long as there is life, there is hope"—so they clung to the canoe the whole of that long, long, never to be forgotten day.

Towards evening as the sun was sinking behind the western hills, the canoe struck bottom near where they had started from in the morning. The Indians immediately came to their rescue. How true the saying that "a friend in need is a friend indeed." The sufferers were so benumbed, that they had no use of their limbs or bodies; not enough to unloosen their grips on the canoe.

Aleck could not stand when the Indians carried him on shore. They were carried to a large fire the Indians had prepared for them. They were made as comfortable as possible under the circumstances. The Indians now set up a howl, and began to mourn the loss of the two warriors who lost their lives in this perilous expedition.[4] We might add many more stirring incidents of Aleck as a trapper, but do not wish to make this part of his life tedious; besides, we will yet relate many adventures he had with wild animals during his life.

[4] In C. A. Menefee's *Historical and Descriptive Sketch Book of Napa, Sonoma, Lake and Mendocino*, p. 284, it is stated that this incident took place on the Yellowstone River, and not the Gulf of California.

CHAPTER III.

Lower California

ALECK, after being rescued from a watery grave, and after recovering from the effects of it, began to wonder what he would do next. He was plucky and full of determination, but his courage now began to flag. Do you blame him, reader? Thrice he had made his fortune, and thrice it had been taken from him when about ready to receive the money and return home. That his fortune did not lay in trapping and hunting was now plainly proven to him. He now had nothing in the world but the suit on his back and only moccasins on his feet. But the greatest loss of all was his favorite friend, his gun, which had stood between him and danger so often, and which had oftentimes kept him from starving.

No gun, no friend, and almost out of hope, he knew not what to do or how to raise another outfit. He had risked his all to make a fortune, and now he had lost. He was now destitute, away from home, and among strangers, and had no means to start with again. But with all these disasters and mishaps, he never once thought of returning home a poor man; he had resolved to return a rich man and unless he could do so, he would never return and show his face among his friends and early associates.

Alexander now concluded to change his vocation and pursue some other calling. He had often heard the fur-traders speak of a fort at the mouth of the Columbia River, and of a trade carried on between that place and Boston. Also of a trade in hide and tallow carried on between Lower California and Boston. As there was no other opening he concluded to go to the Pacific Coast. He struck out for the nearest point, which proved to be San Diego.[1] Here he found several white men busily engaged in tearing up the hull of a wrecked vessel and getting the lumber and plunder ashore. Aleck offered his services and was employed at ($12.00) twelve dollars per month. This enabled him to get some clothing, and he had the satisfaction of being with white men again. He now watched his every opportunity of bettering his condition; he knew he would never make a fortune at $12.00 per month. He now thought it was about time to send word home as he had been away from home four years and had never written home during [this] long period of time.

[1]According to Menefee, Alexander arrived in San Diego in 1827. But Bancroft, in *Register of Pioneer Inhabitants of California* 1542 *to* 1848, A-E, p. 689, states: "the date has been variously given from 1827 to 1835; but original archive evidence of 1837-45 leaves no doubt that he came in 1832 or 1833."

Now from the letter he sent home the reader can form an idea of what he thought of this section of country.

N. B. Please bear in mind that Aleck was a man of few words, and after being from home so long, he had but a few lines to write; notwithstanding, he might have written an interesting volume of his many incidents.

Dear Brother.

My trapping expedition is an entire failure, all lost. I am now in Lower California. I like it here very well; I am not coming home until I make something. I think there is a fortune for me somewhere, and I am going after it. I am well and hearty, think this a better country than Illinois. And will stop here awhile.

Your Brother. Cyrus Alexander.

We next find Aleck engaged in killing Sea Lions and Sea Otters. These animals were killed for the oil only. Aleck and other men now started in this business determined to make it pay. When they began, these animals were quite numerous along the Pacific Coast, and they were enabled to carry on quite an extensive business. The business was quite a change for Aleck. In killing animals he found that they came in and went out with the tide. Any of the stragglers fared roughly when found by Aleck and his companions. Most of these singular animals were surprised and killed on the beach.

The Sea Lions are very heavy and clumsy, and

cannot make much time on land; they neither walk or slide, their principal locomotion seems to be a kind of tumble which costs them much effort. The killing process was a very simple one; the hunter would approach and hit them on the nose or snout with a club.

The Sea Otter required more stratagem; he is pretty sharp and lively and required considerable skill to be captured. They were compelled to watch him cautiously; their only method of capturing him was to shoot him with a rifle and it took good shooting at that; but then Aleck had learned to handle a rifle by this time; it did not make him nervous, even if his life depended on a single shot. Many an unfortunate Sea Otter never moved after he pulled trigger.

As the game began to get scarce and shy, they started for Guadalupe Island; this island is situated off the coast of Lower California, two hundred miles from San Diego, and ninety miles from the Port of San Quintin. This island is twenty six miles long and ten miles wide, containing about 166,400 acres. It is timbered with white pine, is mountainous and picturesque, with a valley extending across the center. Mt. Augusta, the highest point, is 3000 feet above sea level. It is now occupied by the Guadalupe Island Co., who are engaged in raising and breeding Angora Goats. Wm. M. Landrum, Esq. is the president of the company. The Island is to-day valued at $270,000.

On arriving at the island Aleck and Co. found the Sea Lions and Otters more numerous than on the coast.

The climate good, also plenty of good fresh water. Their market was handy; they disposed of their stock to the Hide and Tallow Co. and received cash for all their oil-producing animals. These two animals are quite a sight for those coming here from the Eastern states, and attract considerable attention. The only ones we ever heard of being exhibited in the Eastern states were exhibited by the world's renowned caterer, P. T. Barnum, Esq; and we will add that they were good specimens. The animal in its native element will of course attain a greater size than those owned by Mr. Barnum.

Aleck and Co., in hunting these animals had so much success, that he soon found it necessary to change his business. He slew them by the wholesale, and they soon became scarce, wild, and shy.

We next find Aleck learning the Spanish language. At this time, this section of our union was under the Mexican Government, and the Spanish language was universally spoken. Business could not be conducted without a knowledge of it. So Aleck pitched into the Spanish lingo and learned to speak it quite fluently; of course he made many sad, also ludicrous blunders. "But nothing venture nothing win." He determined to learn it, and when he once got the run of it he soon followed it up. The Spanish language is still very popular; the Digger Indians converse mostly in this language, and many of the young Californians have a smattering of it.

The principal business here at this time was stock raising and the hide and tallow trade, before mentioned, carried on between San Diego and Boston. Among the other traders was one Capt. Fitch,[2] a native of Massachusetts, who was extensively engaged in the live stock business. Fitch had his ships on the seas, and numerous heads of cattle grazing on the extensive valley land granted to him by the Mexican Government.

Capt. Fitch took a liking to our determined, but so far unlucky adventurer, which proved a good thing for him in the end. Aleck made friends wherever he went, but most of them were like himself, poor, and their fortune yet to be made. But Fitch was a wealthy and influential man, able and willing to help the wanderer. The Mexicans were anxious to improve the country, and as Capt. Fitch was an enterprising "yankee" they gave him all the encouragement they could.

The rule of the country at that time was that all who wished to be land-holders had two things to comply with; first to marry a native Spanish Mexican woman; second to swear allegiance to the Mexican Govern-

[2] Henry Delano Fitch was born in 1799 at New Bedford, Mass. He came to California in 1826. He settled in San Diego and was married there in 1829 to Josefa Carrillo, daughter of Don Joaquin Carrillo and sister-in-law of Mariano G. Vallejo, who lived in Sonoma County. In 1841, Captain Fitch was given a grant of three square leagues of land in Sonoma County which later became known as the Sotoyome Rancho. This amounted to about 13,000 acres. He died in San Diego in 1849. "Capt. Fitch was one of the earliest, most prominent and most popular of the early pioneers; straightforward in his dealings, generous in disposition, frank and cheerful in manner." (Bancroft F-H, p. 739.)

ment. As Fitch had complied with both of these exceptions, and being a general favorite, he received large grants of land from them and fared well.

In all newly settled countries if a young man wishes to succeed, he must be industrious and of steady habits, particularly if he does not possess any capital. Aleck did not have very much money, but he was frugal and industrious, ever ready to make himself useful, no matter what the nature of the work was. If one thing did not "pan out" he would try another; he thought he would strike the right "trail" some time.

Aleck, after becoming acquainted with Capt. Fitch, found ready employment, receiving the usual wages then paid, that is from ten to fifteen dollars per month. He worked at this rate for Capt. Fitch for some time, and then changed his vocation again.

We next find him engaged in the soap business. He collected a lot of refuse tallow and went to work with his usual energy. The soil in many parts, in the vicinity of San Diego, was impregnated with alkali so strongly, that by shoveling it into hoppers and draining water through it, the lye would be strong enough for soap manufacturing purposes.

Aleck in telling about the lye said: "If you would just shovel up the ground and pour water on it, it would be lye." We never heard him say much about the alkali, or the cause of it; he knew it would make lye, and this satisfied him. As the ingredients used in the soap business were quite cheap, and some of them could be had for the collecting, he made this business pay. He had a good run of customers, as the Spanish families never made their own soap, but depended entirely on buying, and besides this he had no opposition. Many of the Spanish families did not have much use for soap. But Aleck soon tired of this; he saw he could not make a fortune and so he quit the business.

Aleck now thought if he could become a land owner he could do better. He saw that stock raising was a paying business. But he did not see how he could arrange things; he was not married, and did not like to lose his American Citizenship. Rumors now stated that there was good grazing ground north of San Francisco Bay. Also that there were white settlements there.

Capt. Fitch came to Aleck and said: you go north of the Bay, take a good look at the country, and if you can find enough unclaimed land suitable for a stock range, I will ask it of the Government, and if I can get it I will stock it, and you can run it on shares.

This proposition just suited the adventurer, and with his usual readiness, he soon made the necessary arrangements for the trip. He at this time owned five horses, and selecting the best traveler and the hardiest animal of the lot, he collected the other necessary paraphernalia, consisting of a heavy blanket, a saddle, a pair of large Mexican spurs, and the indispensable lariat (Re-at-ta). He then started for the country north of the Bay.

As there were Mexican settlements along the coast near the Mission posts, he did not need to carry much provision with him. He took a supply of jerked beef to fall back on whenever he should fail to reach a house for food and shelter. He crossed the Bay above the Straits and pushed forward toward Napa Valley. This he found already granted to Yount,[3] Bale[4] and others. So he passed through this valley and headed for the Russian River valley. Here he also found a number of grants and settlements, those of Sonoma, Santa Rosa Ranch,[5] Mark West Ranch,[6] Cooper Ranch,[7] Bodega[8] and others, but north of these further up the river, he found a large and fertile tract still unclaimed, and possessing what he considered all the necessary qualities for a good and extensive Stock Ranch.

This valley contained a good quality of land, and was surrounded by a range of low hills covered with

[3] George C. Yount (1794-1865) was granted the Rancho Caymus in Napa County in 1836, and in 1843, Rancho La Jota, an extension of Caymus. (Bancroft R-Z, p. 783; Cowan, *Ranchos of California*, pp. 25, 42.)

[4] Edward Turner Bale (*c.* 1808-*c.* 1850), a surgeon, grantee in 1841 of Rancho Carne Humana. (Bancroft A-E, p. 708; Cowan, p. 24.)

[5] Rancho Cabeza de Santa Rosa, granted in 1841 to Maria Ignacia Lopez de Carrillo, widowed mother of Francisca Benicia. (Cowan, p. 95.)

[6] San Miguel Rancho, containing 6663 acres at Mark West Springs, granted in 1844 to William Mark West. (Cowan, p. 85.)

[7] Rancho Molina (also known as Rio Ayosoka or Levantahyume), 10½ leagues at Graton, granted in 1836 to Juan Bautista Roger Cooper. (Hoover, Rensch, and Rensch, *Historic Spots in California*, p. 375.)

[8] Rancho Bodega, eight leagues from Bodega Bay to the Russian River, granted in 1841 to Victor Prudon. (Hoover, p. 376.)

timber, and an abundance of good water, numerous springs besides the river and creeks; possessed a good climate. Alexander was highly pleased with his discovery; he was satisfied this would make a good home, and if Capt. Fitch could secure this all would be well.

Aleck sent Capt. Fitch a flattering report of this section of the country. Fitch now applied to the Government, and succeeded in securing a Grant. After arranging the preliminaries, [he] came up to see the tract, and was given possession of the tract, which was known as the Sotoyome[9] Grant, containing eleven Spanish leagues of land.[10]

In the year 1840,[11] Aleck completed his arrangements with Fitch, and took charge of the ranch. He selected a place on the east side of the river as a site for his house and other improvements, just opposite from where the flourishing town of Healdsburg now stands. We will give a short description of his first

[9] Sotoyome: "the home of Soto; i.e., of the chief of a Southern Pomo village near Healdsburg." (Barrett, *The Ethno-geography of the Pomo and Neighboring Indians*, p. 218). According to Josefa Carrillo Fitch, patentee of the grant, the name consists of *sati*, "brave," and *yomi*, "rancheria." (From *Narracion*, a MS in the Bancroft Library.)

[10] According to Cowan, pp. 148 and 151, a league contains "2.633573 miles or 5000 varas, according to the U.S. surveys.... All other authorities checked give the league as 8000 varas.... A square league, (U. S. survey) equals 6.935 plus square miles or about 4438 acres." A vara is a Spanish yard of 33.385 inches or 2.781 feet. The 1841 grant, according to Cowan, p. 100, consisted of eight leagues. Hoover, p. 375, states that the 1841 grant consisted of three leagues, to which eight more were added in 1844.

[11] This date may be in error. The actual grant of the land to Fitch did not take place until September, 1841.

house: in building it he had access to but few tools and no nails; he split and hewed the sidings from the renowned redwood–for which California is noted–this wood is similar to white pine, but not so heavy or close grained; it is easily worked and lasts almost a lifetime.

He cut grooves in the sills and plates, and after framing these, he set the sidings up in the grooves in the sills and placed the plates on top of the sidings and all were firmly held together. The only sawed lumber used was two planks which he afterwards procured at Sonoma; these he used for a door. Every thing that needed binding was bound with rawhide–Californians use bale rope now; civilization is still marching onward.

The nearest town at that time was the Catholic Mission town of Sonoma, about thirty five miles distant. He was compelled to procure all his implements from this place. He now found that he must make a raise of a team of some kind. He soon made a raise of a yoke of Spanish oxen and the primitive carriage which we will describe. The two wheels were sections of a log, with a hole drilled and bored through the center. The axle was a pole sharpened at both ends, for spindles, and with a hole and pin in the end to keep the wheels on. A pole fastened to the center of this answered for a tongue. Upon this frame-work was set, or fastened, a kind of wicker-work composed of sticks and strips of rawhide. This was all it was; a simple arrangement, yet it answered in its day and time. One thing in favor of this vehicle was this: when they mired in the adobe, they could keep turning haw[12] around until they twisted the concern out of the mud.

Aleck owned the second carriage of this denomination in this section of California. The oxen were yoked with a stick across the forehead, notched and crooked, so as to fit the head closely, and tied with rawhide. After Aleck had his team ready for performance, he started on his maiden trip to Sonoma. He arrived there all right, and loaded his cart with such articles as were dispensable in a new settlement; he then hitched up his team and started homeward. He had been delayed considerable, and the rainy season was now at hand. He had been on his home trip, but one day when the rain began to pour down, there was no road and the soil in the valleys was adobe–those who have traveled over wet adobe know how to sympathize with our unfortunate teamster–this adobe is similar to blue clay, and when wet it is very sticky, and adhering to everything. Shortly after dark the wheels began to clog, and soon after refused to turn on the spindle. The oxen sulked; the rain still pouring down left Aleck in anything but a cheerful condition. Some reader may ask, did he swear? We think not; swearing would only make a bad matter worse.

It left him in the middle of the plains, far from home and unable to proceed any further except on foot. He

[12] haw: left.

now unyoked his jaded oxen, covered his flour with the two planks before mentioned and making himself as comfortable as possible under the circumstances, concluded to wait for morning light. Morning came at last and still it rained; he now made up his mind to abandon his cart on the plains (the cart was mired down to the axle), and wait until the storm was over. After the weather cleared up a little, he procured the assistance of some of the natives (Diggers) and at last succeeded in making the first road-trip in a *carriage* from the Russian River to Sonoma and back.

As he was now ready to begin work in good earnest, Mr. Fitch came up to survey the land and take full possession of it, also to draw up a contract with Mr. Alexander. Surveying under the Mexican and the United States rule are two different things. The Mexicans were not so particular as land was plenty. We will give the reader an account of Mexican Surveying. In the first place the lariat was substituted for the chain and the pins were long enough to handle on horseback. All surveying was performed on horseback. The surveyor would set his compass and take the bearing of a high hill or a tree as far as the eye could reach, and then give the word *vamose!* And away they would go on a fast trot and sometimes on a dead run, drawing the pins and setting others while mounted, and not stopping their horses until they had run the line. They would get over a large tract of land in a day. This method of surveying was very imperfect, and has caused many a bitter quarrel and lawsuit in California. Uncle Sam's surveyors find that the Mexicans made too much allowance for wear and tear. Fitch and Aleck now drew up their contract.

The contract in substance was as follows: Fitch was to stock the ranch with horses and cattle, and Aleck was to guard them and take care of them, for the period of four years; at the end of each year, the stock was to be driven up and to be divided, Aleck to have one half of the increase. And at the end of four years, Aleck was to have two leagues of the ranch. They were to *Rodeo* the cattle once a year, that is, to drive them into a corral and brand and divide them.

Before *Rodeoing* the cattle it was customary to send word throughout the vicinity to the different stock raisers, so that each could come and take out his cattle if any were found in the herd. In this way the cattle were prevented from becoming estrays and running wild. When *Rodeoing* they always managed to have a good time; they would select a good beef and kill it, and then feast until it was all gone. All cattle had to be branded; some were branded with the initial of the owner's name, others with the symbol of the ranch.

The rule or law of branding cattle was very strict; if any one branded an animal belonging to some one else and it was found out on him, he had to return fourfold. Aleck was very particular about branding cattle; he wanted to become rich but he wanted to get rich honestly.

Some of the early settlers near Healdsburg who had as good a show as Aleck but did not do so well are jealous of his success, and here of late have been making remarks about him, saying that when Aleck saw an estray in his vicinity, he would take his branding iron and a match, and after catching the animal he would brand it, and in this way he became rich. But these are rumors without any foundation. Aleck never possessed a dollar in the world but what he came by honestly. It is true he had many chances and temptations, but such an idea never occurred to him.

As he was settled now and had to wait for his fortune, he concluded to build a large house. The only material to be had was adobe; there was plenty of good soil near by for this purpose. The only help he could get were the poor degraded Digger Indians, scarcely a grade higher than the brute creation. And as Aleck said, the only difference in their mode of living was that the Digger carried fire and the grizzlies did not.

He built quite an extensive house; they cut the adobe into large oblong pieces, and after being sun dried, piled them up into walls, similar to brick houses. The Diggers carried the adobe and helped him to build his house. This house is still standing on what is called the Fitch Ranch,[13] near Fitch Mountain, and the present town of Healdsburg.[14] It is now occupied by Mrs.

[13] Previously known to the Indians and earlier settlers as *Sotoyome.*

[14] Harmon G. Heald had a trading post at what is now Healdsburg since 1846. He built the first store in town in 1852. (Gudde, *California Place Names*, p. 129).

Capt. Fitch, and has the appearances of lasting for many years yet to come.

Aleck next made preparations to set out an orchard. Hearing that there was an orchard at Fort Ross—a Russian Fort—situated at what is now called Timber Cove, about forty-five miles west of his ranch on the Coast, he sent Frank Bidwell,[15] with a Digger as a guide, to see about an orchard. Frank and the Digger started for the Fort, but did not succeed in reaching it for the first day, so they camped for the night, and renewed their journey early the next morning.

On arriving at the Fort, Frank found an orchard including about an acre, fenced in with hewed redwood planks about two inches thick and fifteen feet high. This fence was intended to keep the Diggers out, they not being very particular about the 8th Commandment. Frank procured the sprouts, and after resting his bronchos and partaking of some substantial grub, he and his guide started homeward; on arriving at Russian River he found it had raised, and that it would be dangerous to attempt to cross it. So he went to work to construct a raft, expecting to swim the bronchos.

He lashed some logs together, pushed it into the stream, and then he and his guide boarded it. They led their bronchos, and were progressing finely, until nearing the opposite shore, when the "raft went back

[15] Bancroft gives the name as Bedwell. Franklin Bedwell was born in Tennessee. After a career as a trapper in the Rocky Mountains, like Cyrus Alexander, he came to California in 1840 or 1841. He bought some property from Cyrus Alexander in 1844. (Bancroft A-E, p. 714.)

on them." Frank, seeing that he could navigate no further on the raft, thought he would abandon it, but before he could make the necessary preparations, the raft parted, and he and the Digger fell into the river.

They now struck out for terra firma, and both being good swimmers, they soon reached the shore in safety. They now concluded to hunt a place where they could remain over night, dry their clothing, and get some grub. Not finding such a place they camped out. Early the next morning they came to an Indian hut, but all the grub it contained was an *abolona* (a kind of clam); the Indians prepared this, and it did not take Frank and his guide long "to get away with it."

Frank now hurried on, as he thought he would stop at the house of a Mr. Smith,[16] on the way, and get some grub there, but on arriving there, he found Smith out of provision excepting a few apples, partly rotted, which Smith had brought from the Fort. Smith was soon relieved of his apples, and Frank saw no more show for grub, until he should arrive at home, which he did that evening. Aleck was glad to get the sprouts, and he soon prepared a substantial meal, so that Frank and his guide were soon enjoying "solid comfort." Aleck planted the sprouts and peach seeds; this was in 1843; they flourished, and the orchard is still in a good bearing condition; the trees are large and thrifty.

[16] Possibly Stephen Smith, owner of Rancho Bodega on the Russian River. He first came to California in 1841 and died in 1855. (Bancroft R-Z, p. 724; Hoover, p. 376.)

Aleck rewarded the Diggers by killing game for them, and by always fulfilling his promises to them he gained their good will, and could get them to assist him whenever he wished their services. The Diggers speak a Spanish lingo, and as Aleck now spoke the Spanish fluently, he got along with them without any difficulty. They built their huts and sweat houses near him. As many of my young readers would like to know what a sweat house is we will tell you.

The Diggers live on Rancherias—a small town on a ranch. Their sweat-houses are built near the streams. They dig down into the ground some distance, and then build a house around this hole, of adobe perfectly airtight, and shaped like a bee-hive tapering into a point, with a small hole in the top to emit the smoke; they leave a hole just large enough to crawl through, and arranged so that it can easily be closed.

On certain occasions they go to their sweat-houses, build a large fire, then strip until perfectly nude—they do not have much to strip—and go in; while in the sweat-house they gamble until the perspiration almost overcomes them; in this warm and heated condition, they come out, and plunge into the cold water. Do not let this shock you, Gentle Reader; perhaps you think this would kill a human being. But remember the Diggers do not live, act, or look like human beings. And we really doubt whether they can lay any claims to humanity. Besides, "it depends altogether on how a person is brought up."

A man in Napa Valley was digging a well on what was once an old Rancheria; on digging down several feet, he discovered that the ground was greasy or oily; he at once came to the conclusion that it was a spot where a sweat-house had once stood, and that the Diggers had perspired until the grease had run down and soaked the ground. But as we will again refer to the "Noble Red Man," we will continue with Mr. Alexander.

CHAPTER IV.

A Home at Last

PERHAPS many a young American would not have accepted the situation that Mr. Alexander did, as it was then not known if this section of the country would ever amount to anything or not. The outlook was that it would remain a "harum-scarum" stock raising country, and that only for the "Hide and Tallow Business."

But Aleck was tired of roving and wanted to settle down some where; he was determined to give this business a fair trial, and besides this he was now in honor bound, and he must perform. His young orchard grew and prospered; he now purchased and sowed some wheat, and was agreeably surprised at his first crop. He now felt satisfied that California would grow wheat to perfection—we will refer to wheat again. He said that everything he now worked at proved a success.

He surely deserved success; he had met with failures enough; misfortune had followed him and clung to him in all his previous undertakings. He spent much of his leisure time in tramping over the surrounding hills, always carrying his rifle with him for safety and procuring meat, also for killing such wild animals as would molest his young stock. There were plenty of these kind of animals here in those days, such as Grizzly and other bears, panthers, coyotes, wild-cats, catamounts etc. But recently, 1875, a Grizzly bear was killed within a few miles of Alexander's home–wild cats are quite common yet. Aleck was a good hunter and a cool deliberate shot, as the following incident will show. We will give his own words.

"I was out one afternoon on Dry Creek; it was quite warm, and I felt it was a good time to see a bear; sure enough, I had not been out long when I saw a large Grizzly feeding on the clover; I concluded to have him if possible. There was a large white oak near him. I crept quietly up to this and stood watching the old fellow; soon I had a good chance and fired. Down he tumbled, making a terrible fuss. I stood still, looking at him; suddenly he rose up, sitting on his hind parts, and trying to find where his enemy was. I could not load again for fear he would see me; suddenly he came down on his feet and made straight for the tree; as he came up on one side, I stepped around, thus keeping out of sight. He came near enough to the tree to stumble over its roots, and so near to me that I could see him wink. Not seeing anything he passed on. That was one time I did not shoot hard enough, and so lost my game. It did not matter much as I soon found another which I killed."

In this way two years passed quite pleasantly, that is, if pleasure can be found in solitude. Aleck had been away from civilization so long that it was no trouble for him to amuse himself. Work will make time pass, if nothing else will. Aleck now concluded to replenish his wardrobe; of course he did not use kid gloves and broadcloth; he wanted something more substantial than these, something that would stand the wear and tear of his rough and tumble occupation.

In order to manufacture wearing apparel, he found it necessary to start a tannery–one of his early occupations. He found a good location on Fitch Mountain, which would answer his purpose admirably. His will was his aid, and his power to do his capital; with these for a beginning, he sunk his vats and went to work. The bark he obtained in the near vicinity; the hides were also easy to obtain, but when he wanted lime, he found himself at a loss. He now sent some of his Digger friends to the coast, distant about thirty five miles, to bring sea-shells in their baskets.

These he burned in a kiln, and was surprised to find what an excellent quality of lime could be obtained from them. This was the first tannery in California north of the Bay. The first leather he tanned proved a success. He was now enabled to make his own shoes and numerous other articles.

Aleck, now having leisure time, concluded he would form the acquaintance of his neighbors; none of them however lived near him. They were as follows; Mr.

Cooper[1] of Bodega, Mark West,[2] living between him and Sonoma, Bale and Yount of Napa Valley, still further north Mr. Gordon[3] of Cache Creek, and east of all of these Capt. Sutter of Sacramento. Gold was first discovered on Sutter's grant years afterward.

Of the above named, Mr. Gordon was most frequently visited for two obvious reasons; first, Gordon had been a Rocky Mountain hunter and trapper, though not at the same time that Aleck was. And as both had been adventurers, they had many a pleasant chat about hunting, etc. Mr. Gordon, after his trapping expedition, went to New Mexico; here he married a Spanish Mexican woman, and after a few years immigrated to California, bringing his wife's sister, a young woman just entering her teens, with him. This was his second and principal attraction, and you may safely vouch it had considerable influence over him.

The two grants, Fitch and Gordon, were situated about one hundred miles apart. And as it was no small

[1] John Bautista Roger Cooper (1792-1872). Born in Alderney. Grantee of the Rancho Molina, Sonoma. (Bancroft A-E, p. 765.)

[2] William Mark (or Marcus) West (*c.* 1796-*c.* 1850), grantee of the Rancho San Miguel. Mark West Creek in Sonoma is named after him. (Bancroft R-Z, p. 772.)

[3] William Gordon (1801-1876). Born in Ohio, he married Maria Lucero, whose sister later became Mrs. Cyrus Alexander, and came to California in the Rowland-Workman party in 1841. After coming north to Sonoma in 1842, he became the grantee the following year of the Quesesosi Rancho on Cache Creek, thereby becoming the pioneer settler of Yolo County. Between 1843 and 1846, his place was a general rendezvous for settlers and hunters, and with the exception of Sutter's Fort and Sonoma, is more frequently mentioned than any other place. (Bancroft F-H, p. 762.)

matter to make these trips, Aleck hurried things up as much as possible. Aleck did all his courting, wooing, cooing, billing, etc., in the Spanish language. He did not stop to fool. His courtship was short; he dispensed with the flirting, grinning, swinging on the gate, and fol-de-rol so common at the present day. He meant business. His motto was "faint heart never won fair lady." She smiled on his suit, and with the consent of Mr. Gordon, he and Miss Ruphena Lucerne[4] were married by Capt. Sutter in December 1844.

A better choice he could not have made, as she was "cut out" for a pioneer's wife. He now had a help-mate that was a help-mate in reality. She seemed to understand her position as the wife of a new beginner in a new country, and whatever may be said of the *first women* of California, Mrs. Cyrus Alexander was a good, true, and worthy woman. She was ever ready to assist her husband, never stopping to murmur over the many drawbacks that were subjected to house-keeping in those early days. After the marriage at Capt. Sutter's, they spent a short time at Mr. Gordon's in having a merry time, the last thing on the programme being a good old fashioned dance. After this they bade their friends good-bye, and started for their home near the Russian River, which they reached in safety, after a three day's ride, arriving there at night. No one to welcome the bride to her new home. She had no com-

[4] Rufina Lucero (May 1830-March 16, 1908). Sister of Maria Lucero (Mrs. William Gordon). (Gregory, *History of Sonoma County*, p. 794.)

pany but her husband for years, as women did not come to this part of California until years afterward.

Mr. Alexander now had some one depending on him for support; he had some one to love, some one to cherish. He now worked with renewed energy; he improved the place and gave it a home like appearance. The stock business was now increasing every day. As there was considerable stock on the ranch and on others in the same vicinity, the "Hide and Tallow" Trade was now getting to be quite an extensive business. And consequently the country was visited by people seeking employment, as slaughtering the cattle now required help. Many came to look at the country in search of homes, and as an increase of people makes an increase of trade, Aleck enlarged his tannery and tanned leather for saddles, leggins, shoes, etc.

He sent his leather to market at Sutter's Fort. There was now a great demand for cigaritas, and obtaining the material for these through the influence of Capt. Fitch, he and his wife manufactured great numbers of these. So we now have Aleck as a Cigar-maker. The smoking of cigaritas is greatly indulged in; every body smokes cigaritas. The cigaritas of to-day are made as follows: the smoking population of California carry brown paper—common straw paper—, plug tobacco, and a knife. They tear the paper in strips about two and a half inches long, and an inch and a quarter wide; they then cut some tobacco up fine and roll it up in this. Practice makes them quite skilful in rolling up these cigaritas. The cigarita business was quite profitable to Aleck; if there was any money in the country, he was determined to have his share of it.

As trade called people here and houses were scarce, his house being the furthest from civilization in this direction, he concluded to put up another house. It was understood between Fitch and himself that he was to be paid for all improvements. So employing some of his Digger friends to make adobe, he went to work at his new house. Communication now being more frequent and sure, he was enabled to get carpenter tools and other materials for his house. So this house was actually finished with doors and windows, similar to the houses in his native state. This building is still standing and occupied; thus you see that Aleck owned and used the first carpenter tools in Sonoma County, California. In order to show the perfect confidence between Fitch and Aleck, we will give you the substance of a letter from Fitch to Aleck.

San Diego, July 14th 1845

Mr. Cyrus Alexander
Dear Sir.

Yours of March 25th I did not receive until the 27th of last month. I am sorry to learn that you intend to leave the Rancho in October next, consequently I have made arrangements with Mr. Moses Carson to take charge of the Rancho, with all my interest in the same; and have given him orders to that effect. Whatever articles I sent you, such as farming utensils, carpenter tools etc, that you do not wish to keep, I will take back at the same price, provided they are not too much damaged by wear. The two large whalers' tripods, the winnowing machine, and the American cart wheels I never considered as sold to you, but delivered them to be used on the rancho. I expect you to leave them, also the large auger, Grist mill spindle and tire, logchain, screw-plates, and other Iron-and-steel ware sent in 1843, too numerous to mention, such as locks, hinges etc. I told Mr. Carson that in case you wished to deliver anything he considered not receivable, to give you a receipt, and to retain them as on deposit. I hope you have received the 300 head of cattle from Pico, and those from Marco Baco and Pacheva [Pacheco?] *and have taken them to your part of the Rancho; in that case you will deliver all of my cattle to Mr. Carson, and I will settle all differences when I come up. There were 250 head of sheep; after making the old stock good, you will please divide the increase, and deliver my share to Mr. Carson; you will also deliver to him one half of the wool, and one half of all the grain raised. I have been disappointed in not receiving a letter from you sooner; you said nothing about the crops. You stated that you had sent me fifteen fanagas,*[5] *one of*

[5] Fanega: approximately one bushel.

beans, eight of wheat. I expected more beans and corn, and I have not received even that small lot. There must be some neglect somewhere. I have not had a bean in my house for two months. I requested Mr. Carson to ship me some from the Rancho in case there were any there. You will please advise and assist Mr. Carson; in so doing you will oblige me. As to the new house, I hope you have the walls up, and as to the boards and shingles, I do not care to engage any more, but will attend to that myself. Wishing you every success, I remain, *Yours Truly*

H. D. Fitch.

P. S. According to my account, I have forwarded to you from Nov. 1841 to Nov. 1843 the following number of cattle viz: 39 oxen, 4 tame cows, 149 cows de rodeo, 468 barquates,[6] *large and small, 45 nobeds,*[7] *64 bulls, 65 barquas,*[8] *88 head of cattle from Raphel Garcio; Mr. Leice [Leese] delivered 922 head; Mr. Larkins delivered some since. In 1842 I put 22 tame horses, 3 tame mares, 4 wild mares, 4 macheos,*[9] *and 1 colt. I have the papers of the Rancho approved by the assembly, and think all will be correct.*

Respectfully H. D. Fitch.

[6] Probably *baquitas* or *vaquitas:* heifers.
[7] *Novillos:* young bulls or oxen.
[8] *Bacas* or *vacas:* cows.
[9] *Machos:* mules.

The American cart wheels mentioned in the letter were the first of the kind used in Sonoma County.

All things now being satisfactorily settled between the two men, Aleck was now a free man again. He had faithfully performed and fulfilled his part of the contract, and had received his reward. Providence had favored him at last. His land was part of the Sotoyome Grant, lying on the east side of the Russian River, including the land from the river's channel to the line of the said Grant, along the foothills north and east far enough to include two Spanish leagues. He received his title and deed September 2nd, 1847.

All of his labor here-after was to be performed on his own land; he was now a land owner; he now had a good Ranch, plenty of work on hand, as it was wild unimproved land, and contained good valley, timber, and hill ground, and streams of living water. He now began to move his stock and effects to his own property. He still owned and used the primitive carriage with which he had made the trip to Sonoma. This institution he repaired so he could make use of it in moving his effects; he strapped his oxen to it, and with the aid of some pack-horses succeeded in getting his personal property, with his wife and child, to his new, and as he hoped, his permanent home.

Mr. Alexander was now 40 years old,[10] and during the most of his life, as the reader is aware of, he had had nothing but temporary homes; several years of

[10] Cyrus Alexander was actually 42 years old at this time.

his life had been spent in camping in unexplored, and what is still an unsettled region. His manly heart must have beat with pride when he placed his foot on his own ground, to be a weary wanderer no more.

He had toiled, waited, hoped, dreamed and struggled on until at last, success had crowned him. The best part of his life had been spent in trying to reach this point; although bitter reverses and opposition had stared him in the face at nearly everything he had undertaken, he persevered until he had conquered. His determination, pluck, and grit had been tried again and again; the only time he was really discouraged with his lot was when he had lost his all in trying to cross the Gulf.

He chose for a building spot a small eminence over which a large stream of spring water flowed from a large hill above, and still further up, a little to the east, was a number of springs forming quite a brook, which flowed down to the valley below like a silver thread, sparkling on its way and seeming to cheer and encourage our hero with his work.

He often said that this was, and seemed to him, the brightest and best spot in the world. Do you blame him for thinking so, my reader? The valley and hills were covered with grass and clover, and was tall enough [for the stock] to hide themselves in. Here in this lovely place he encamped, under a large spreading live-oak tree, until he could build a temporary house for shelter. Making adobe, or sun dried bricks, was slow work. So he concluded to erect a redwood cabin for shelter until time and help could assist him in putting up a large and more substantial house.

Large forests of redwood were near, and as these trees split free, easy and straight, he concluded to build his cabin of this species of wood. It has often been stated, and the rising generation are aware of the gigantic growth of these large trees, one of them being large enough to furnish material enough to build a house from sill to shingle, make the furniture, etc., and then furnish rails or pickets for fencing several acres of land, and then still have some remaining for fire-wood. Hundreds of sawmills are now at work sawing up these large and useful trees; these trees are the wonder of California. And as many other writers have given many useful and truthful accounts of them, we will only mention them when necessity calls for them.

In erecting his cabin, Aleck split the redwood into slabs and fastened them similar to the first cabin on the Fitch part of the Rancho. He used the ground for a floor and an old fashioned fire place for a stove. After getting his family comfortably situated, he began to till the ground. The first crop he intended to put in was wheat, and as he now needed a plow, he went to work to make one.

Selecting a long piece of timber for a beam, he fastened a handle on one end of it, and then chiseled out a mortise to admit the plow, which was a short stick with a natural crook with a small piece of iron fastened on one end of it. To this comical instrument he attached his oxen, and so long as he could hold it up, it would root up considerable. This was one of the pioneer plows of California. Aleck never took out a patent on his invention. He plowed up a field and sowed his wheat, using a brush instead of a harrow to drag it under with. He procured his seed wheat from Chile.

As he had no method of getting rails to his ranch, he built a brush fence and hired some of the Diggers to guard his crop for him. He paid them in wheat, generally managing to get them interested in the crop. It was no trouble for the Diggers to scare away the cattle, as the cattle were naturally afraid of them, and would run if they saw or only scented a Digger. The cattle seemed to fear the Diggers as much as they did the Grizzly bears. Besides this, good grazing grass grew rich and abundantly along the streams, and as it was near the water, they did not bother much.

When the wheat was ready for harvest, it was harvested with a sickle which Aleck had brought from San Diego. The threshing was quite a different thing from from what it is to-day. Steam threshing machines were then unknown. Threshing was quite a performance for one just from the land "of steady habits." The corral into which they drove the horses and cattle to lasso them, after a while became quite hard; into this they would pile up the grain and then the *manatha*,[11]

[11] *Manada.*

or band of mares were turned upon it to tramp out the grain. They would select the wildest horses—or those which were driven up but once a year to brand the colts—upon this wheat; they would drive them round and round, crosswise and every other wise, until the grain was trampled out of the head. The horses were wild and did not need much urging as a general thing.

After treading, the wheat would be a mass of grain and chaff. This was the only method of threshing known in California at that time, as Aleck left Illinois in 1830, and as they then threshed with horses on the barn floor, or beat it out with flails, threshing machines being then unknown. He had never seen a threshing machine. The most difficult part of the operation was separating the grain from the chaff. As the dry season in California lasts from the middle of May until the middle of October, they had plenty of time to work at the wheat. So when the wind was high enough, the Diggers would toss the mass up into the air with large wooden forks, and the wind would separate it for them.

In some localities the wind was so unsteady that separating would be on hand for months at a time. But when the wind was fair they would clean several bushels in a day, and clean it well; of course, at the present time, we cannot see how they could have the patience to manage things in such a manner; but then, wheat was not raised by the millions of bushels as it is to-day.

The berry of the wheat was then much larger and heavier than it is to-day, and did not contain smut, cheat, thistles and other impurities as it does at the present time.

Little did Aleck think at that time that his ranch would at some future day yield from 25 to 55 bushels of wheat per acre, and that a 44-inch cylinder steam threshing machine would thresh from 1000 to 2500 bushels of wheat per day at 4 cents per bushel. Little did he think when he was trying to plow with his *patent* but home *rooter* that *three* gang plows would plow in the same *land* on his ranch as they did last season, 1875. Or that at some future day, not far distant, steam plows would *root* up the same soil.

While Aleck was busy with his out-door work, improving his ranch, building fences, stables, etc. his wife was busy with her household work in preparing food and clothing for her little family. It was quite amusing to see her spin. Spinning in early days was an institution considered necessary for every family, that is, farmer families, and many different methods were resorted to, but the one pursued by Mrs. Alexander was different from any we [have] ever heard of, or seen.

She had procured some *rolls* from San Diego, and whenever she had leisure time, she would busy herself with spinning these *rolls* into yarn. Her method of spinning may have been primitive, and it may have been an invention of her own; at any rate, it was the first and only method of the kind we ever witnessed.

She had a large earthen bowl, very smooth on the inside; this bowl she would place in her lap while sitting on a low chair. In this bowl she twisted a spindle with her thumb and finger; said spindle was a stick whittled in such a shape as to whirl readily on one end, similar to a boy's top; while keeping this in motion with one hand, she would *pay* out the wool with the other. In this manner she could spin enough yarn in one day for a pair of socks.

Aleck now began to build a loom thinking he would be all right then. He made his own shoes, and if he could manufacture cloth now, as his wife could make the stockings, they would soon have a *whole* suit of clothes, and get along famously. He built the loom and had its various parts completed, but was not able to get a reed, as there were none in the country at this time. And as the Revolution broke out–which we will soon speak of–Alexander had to give up the project.

Some may ask, why did he not have his blankets, clothing material, etc. sent to him by water from the Eastern states? But let such remember that money was not so plentiful as it is now, and that our hero had no money to pay for them, had such a thing been possible.

We will now see what Aleck was driving at in the Spring of 1846. In the Spring of this year, he planted some grape vines, also apple and peach seeds; as soon as they began to grow, he fenced and irrigated them.

At that time it was thought that all fruit trees had to be irrigated. Time and experience has taught the people different. As it was essential to keep leather on hand, he concluded to move his tannery to his own ranch. It took time and hard work to move his tannery, and still more to bring the shells from the ocean, and to collect bark for tanning. Tanning is now carried on quite extensively in California.

As he now wanted more house room, he began to build his last house and future residence. So during the dry season he put up part of the present house and covered it with shingles, packing the shingles from the redwoods on horseback, and hauling them in his cart drawn by oxen. In starting this house, he began it with heavy walls, using nothing but adobe, but we will pass it by, as we will speak of it again. He used this house for various purposes. Part of it was used for a store room for wheat, part for stowing away wool, leather, etc., and part of it was occupied by Frank Bidwell.

Frank Bidwell[12] came to Alexander in 1843 in search of labor; as Aleck had been without the company of white folks so long, he employed Frank, as much for company sake as for the work he might do. Bidwell was a native of Missouri, and "filled the bill" if ever a Missourian did. Aleck made the following proposition to Bidwell. If Bidwell would remain with him 2 years, help to work, etc., Aleck was to give him five hundred acres of land. Bidwell accepted the terms and

[12] See note, p. 45.

remained with him until 1850, and then received his reward.

Frank is still living upon the same five hundred acres of land, and has one of the most handsome dwelling houses in his vicinity. He has his place well improved and fitted up nicely; he has a fine barn, water works, orchard, yard, etc. He has since purchased about eight hundred acres more; his land is nearly all hills, and his principal occupation is sheep raising and fruit. He is considered wealthy. He is a very large and stout man, and may last another generation. We recently learned that he intended to have his life written up, but whether in book form or only for the *Santa Rosa Democrat*, we are unable to say.

Up to this time (1847) Aleck had depended for importation for all his flour, and it made quite a bill in times when money was very scarce in California. As civilization advanced and as wheat grew and prospered so well, Aleck came to the conclusion that California might manufacture her own flour. He felt confident that the California wheat would make as good flour as could be produced any where. The first thing on the programme now was to get a mill. The only way he could see how to manage this was to build one.

So he now resolved to build a mill, and with him to resolve was to do. He found some rock a little east of–now Healdsburg–that he thought would do for millstones, but they were up in the mountains and hard to get at. He hired a Spaniard to cut out the millstones for him; they were about two feet in diameter, and with the aid of a horse and lariat he managed to drag them to a place he could get at them with his cart, and finally succeeded in getting them to the place he had selected for his mill site. This was on the stream before mentioned near his dwelling-house.

The timber for the frame work and roof of the mill he procured near the redwoods. He soon had the frame work ready to set up the machinery, the water wheel being about the size of a wash tub, with arms for the water from a large discharge sluice, from the dam above to strike against. Set in this wheel, and perpendicular with the arms, was the main shaft, and on the upper end of this the spindle–we think the one mentioned in the Fitch letter–and this spindle was connected by a trundle to the stone.

The stream only furnished water enough to run the mill during the rainy season. It was strange to see how this little pioneer mill would turn out flour of the very best quality, sufficient for family use and some to spare to the neighboring ranchers when they called for it. Aleck was neither selfish or jealous, and was always ready to divide with his neighbors. The mill was not large enough to admit of a bolting cloth, if such a thing could have been thought of, but bolting-cloths were then among the things unknown in California. And to send to the states for one was out of the question.

He did at last contrive to make a raise of one; it was

a piece about five feet long and one foot wide. This he stretched on a frame. He then made a box suitable for this frame, with a slide made of slats for the bolting-frame to slide to and fro upon. Thus he was enabled to manufacture bolted flour. He now supplied himself and brother ranchers with as good a quality of flour as any country in the known world could turn out. And we doubt if ever a queen ate sweeter and better bread than Mrs. Alexander made from this flour.

She now had a good brick oven in which to bake her bread. The brick Aleck got as he did almost everything else, that is, he went to work and made them. He first manufactured a pair of brick-molds, in which he moulded the bricks. He also built a lime-kiln in which to burn the sea shells for lime. These shells he had to bring from the Coast, and he could not afford to waste them. The lime-kiln was made of adobe.

Perhaps some of my readers by this time are beginning to think that Aleck could manufacture almost everything. He evidently seemed to be cut out for a Pioneer. His motto must have been–"Where there is a will there is a way." He had led a solitary life, and had to depend on his own ingenuity so long that he was not afraid to undertake anything.

We claim that Aleck built and ran the first mill in the Russian River Valley; also that he made the first brick-kiln, and burnt the first brick in this section of the country; also that he burnt the first lime, and that he built the first tannery and tanned the first leather in what is today called Sonoma County, California. We do not wish to claim a single iota that does not belong to him, nor do we wish to give him any honor belonging to another. He was loved and respected by all who knew him, and if any one knows any thing to the contrary about him, we are willing to acknowledge it before the reading world.

During all this time, from 1834 to 1847, Alexander had been a subject under the Mexican Government, and strange as it may seem to some, he had never given up his American Citizenship. The Mexican Government was now soon to be changed; it had been a very careless Government to some of its subjects in some respects, and in other respects it had been very arbitrary. Aleck had always found it best to acquiesce; it was not for him in his solitude and unaided by any one to rebel.

So far as land was concerned, the Government had dealt very liberally with Aleck; he now owned a large and fertile ranch which would soon be worth a fortune to him. But now the Government made a demand which aggravated him very much; it caused him much trouble, and even made our cool and deliberate hero swear; it was unjust and called forth the indignation of all parties concerned. We are sure that had many of our independent readers been in his place they would have felt just as he did about the matter.

There were several couples married about the same time that Aleck was, and to make things sure, so that no trouble could arise in the future, they made inquiries, and so far as they could find out all was right. They asked Capt. Sutter, who was an *Alcalda*,[13] or Justice of the peace under the Mexican Government, if he had the power to unite them in matrimony, legally and lawfully, so that no dispute could ever arise in the future. He replied in broken English, "Oh yesh, I ish der law, I cans performs der serremony, und all ish den right."

So the parties were married as before stated. Alexander and others were notified from the Catholic Priest at the Catholic Mission town of Santa Clara that they were not legally married, and that they were living together in concubinage, and that the women must return to their parents until proper arrangements could be made for them all to come to Santa Clara and be remarried. That is, be married by the proper authorities, the Catholic Priests.

Alexander [often] spoke of this affair as a "bitter pill," and a hard task for him to perform, but what was he to do! The Priests at that time were a power in California, and he thought it best to give in. He thought the reason the priests had for making this demand was simply because they had received no money from him for his previous marriage. He did not think there was any justice in it; if there was, he never lived to see it in that light. If their object was money, they carried their point, because they received it. Yes, they took the last dollar these poor hard-struggling,

[13] *Alcalde.*

hard-working, self-sacrificing pioneers had worked and toiled for so long.

At this time of life Aleck was in the habit of using very strong language when excited and angered. No one who knew him in Illinois, or who knew him in after life, would ever have thought it possible for him to use such language as he did. And this particular order of the Priests always angered him more than any thing else that ever befell him in his struggles and triumphs. He at the time could not speak of it without uttering an oath. In speaking of it to me he said, "The d——d old shave pates, to put us all to that trouble; it was just the money they were after. They ought to go to H–ll; if the devil don't get them, I don't see what use there is for a devil." It made him swear like a trooper.

It was a difficult thing in those days to get wearing apparel suitable for such occasions. Material for clothing was scarce, money was scarce, and our unfortunate hero found him[self] in a very difficult position. Aleck picked out some of his best leather, and selecting his best fitting lasts, he went to work to make his past-present-and-future wife a pair of new shoes. And fitting up as good a wedding suit as they could muster at the time, in company with some more of the unfortunate ones, they started on their wedding trip to the Mission at Santa Clara on horseback, the distance being about one hundred and twenty miles.

Here the question was asked, did it cost anything.

"Of course it did. I had not spent any money for some time and was laying by what little I could get, as there was not much money in the country, and had saved about $300, and it took it all; and worse than all, it declared my first born illegitimate. You had better believe, if I had had any idea that the Government would change so soon, I should not have gone a step. But what could I do; here I was alone under the Priest's rule, with Indians, and I thought it not safe to rebel."

Three other couples who were married about the same time received the same orders. They were as follows: * * * * * *,[14] Wells Kilburn,[15] and Nathan Coombs.[16] The first two couples accompanied Aleck on his wedding expedition. Mr. Coombs remained at home. Coombs afterward, when meeting with any of the other parties, would always tease and torment them, and make his brags over the affair, saying: "I did not declare by my acts that I thought the first ceremony illegal, and I was confident there would soon be a change in the Government."

Of course Coombs was only guessing at this, as he knew no more about the change of Government coming so soon than did Aleck or any of the rest of the

[14] In the original manuscript, there is a blank space here, probably for later insertion of a name, but the space remains blank.

[15] Probably Ralph L. Kilburn (1809-1879), who settled in Napa County in 1842. (Bancroft I-Q, p. 700.)

[16] Nathan Coombs (*c.* 1824-1877). Settled in Napa County in 1842 and laid out the town of Napa on his rancho. (Bancroft A-E, p. 764.)

parties. Some people are naturally sharp and know every thing after it has happened.

Aleck and the others say that the reason Coombs did not accompany them was simply because he had no shoes for him and his wife to wear, and could not afford to get married a second time. He had a hide in Aleck's tannery, but as it was unfinished at the time, and he did not wish to get married bare-footed, and the others would not wait for him, he was left at home only *once* married. But be that as it may, Coombs and his wife are both living at the present time in Napa City, California and are quite wealthy; he is now able to buy all the shoes he wishes.

Arriving at Santa Clara the Priests made it their business to find out how much money the parties had, and as a matter of course it would cost just as much as they had and were able to pay. Aleck had three hundred dollars, therefore it cost him $300; had he possessed $500 it would have cost him $500. After they were all married a second time, and *married enough* to please all the priests at large and every body else in the world, they made preparations to start for home.

They had a pleasant journey on their *wedding tour*, and in the enjoyment of the trip, they became somewhat mollified. It was "a bitter pill but the doctors said they must swallow it." They concluded to make the best of it, and have as good a time as possible. They all went together and managed to have a lively time. Perhaps this may sound strange, that a party of married folks should go on a wedding tour without money, but then the priest had the money so the *law* was satisfied. The Rainy Season was now on hand, and they had quite a rainy trip part of the way. They stopped one night with Wells Kilburn, who at that time lived in quite a respectable shanty on the banks of Napa Creek. He is at the present time living in Calistoga; fortune did not smile on Kilburn, like it did on the other parties. During the night the rain increased, and Napa Creek flooding its banks, the water ran into the shanty, causing the inmates to get up and raise the floor, in order to keep from getting wet. Next morning, however, the rain abated, and the rest of the party journeyed homeward. Aleck arrived at home the same evening. He next found himself in trouble with the struggle for freedom. California now concluded to throw off the Mexican yoke. Aleck of course was in favor of Freedom.

CHAPTER V.

California Strikes for Freedom

IN THE latter part of the year 1847 and the early part of the year 1848, this wild and almost uncivilized country of the Pacific Coast was thrown into a great excitement. General Castro[1] soon had his hands full; when Americans begin to fight, they mean business. J. C. Fremont with a band of men was out here surveying and exploring the Mountain Regions. He was chosen a leader by the American people of California. He captured the Fort at Sonoma and took General Vallejo prisoner. He raised the Stars and Stripes over the Fort. These disturbances affected the whole country.

The Indians siding with the Mexicans began their depredations as only Indians know how to murder, scalp, torture, and burn and destroy property; it almost appears that Indians were created for this purpose. The Indians began their part of the contest by running off

[1]General Jose Castro (*c.* 1810-1860), commander of Mexican forces in California. (Bancroft A-E, p. 751.)

cattle, stealing grain, etc., and at night would prowl around the houses, not daring to show themselves within range of the rifles.

Alexander was no slouch at handling his rifle, nor would he hesitate if necessity call on him to shoot. The ranchers protected their houses as much as they could with wooden shutters made of live-oak; the arrows of the Indians had but little effect on these. It was very plain to see what the intentions of the Indians were, as arrows could be found lying loose around the house in the morning. Mr. Alexander himself feared nothing; he had dealt with Indians before, but he had a family to protect and care for, and as there was no telling how soon they would or might be overpowered, he concluded to move his family to Fort Sonoma for safety.

This he did as quietly as possible so that the Indians should not find out that he was going to flee. He saddled two horses, and placing his wife and child on one horse, he and a little girl–a niece to his wife–mounted the other; they left the ranch in the evening, and next morning they reached the Fort in safety. This was a proud and happy day for Aleck; once more Freedom's Banner floated over his head, and his country's flag promised him protection.

He was now once more under the protection of the American Government, after being so long with no protection but his good right arm and his trusty and tried rifle. He had been among the savages and wild animals so long that he knew how to appreciate protection; a new feeling arose in his manly bosom. He now knew what it was to live in a free country. All the boys dressed in blue were his friends, and would fight for him to the bitter end. He had endured many hardships among the Indians, and starvation among the Rocky Mountains. And now the Indians with whom he had always dealt fairly had turned upon him. But why should he fear; our National Banner floated over his head and he said: Oh, I can now enjoy a good rest without fear of being overpowered by a lurking enemy.

The reader is well aware that communication had no rapid means of reaching the states in those early days. *The Great Union Central Pacific Rail Road,*[2] the longest Rail Road in the world, the pride of the United States, and the envy of every country under the rays of the sun, did not then connect the "Western Wilds" to Civilization. No, the *Iron horse* did not snort across the plains in five and a half days as he now does. The first communication that Aleck sent home was the short letter before mentioned; this he sent home through the Trading Posts, from Santa Fe to St. Louis. He had then been from home four years and as the trappers seldom had writing material, the word sent home was from the company, and not from the absent one personally, who was so near and dear to the parents, brothers, and sisters at home.

Alexander's family in Illinois were surprised to

[2] See Howard, *The Great Iron Trail*, p. 163.

hear that the wanderer was yet alive and wandering among uncivilized beings in quest of a fortune. But from that time no further communication passed between them until this year, that is, from 1834 to 1848. Alexander had left his home in 1830, and as yet, had not heard from home.

When J. C. Fremont started out on his great Western Exploring Expedition, two of Alexander's nephews were with him. It so happened that this same company were sent to guard the same Fort in which Aleck and his family had taken refuge. That is, the Fort of Sonoma. Most of the families in the Fort, of course, came from the Eastern states. N. B. Californians call all states east of the Rocky Mountains Eastern states. The two nephews were named William Hughes and Risdon A. Moore.[3] They are both living at the present time. The writer met Moore in Belleville some time since; he is rich and is now residing in Belleville, St. Clair County, Illinois.

Hughes and Moore recognized Alexander by his family resemblance and made themselves known to him at once. It was a glad day for Aleck; all can imagine how he felt. It was the first news he had received from home. The first news he had received for eighteen long, long years. Eighteen long years since he had heard from his family; should he dare ask how they all fared? One of his first questions was: How is my

[3] Both Hughes and Moore came to California in the Fremont expedition of 1845. (Bancroft F-H, p. 790; I-Q, p. 744.)

mother, is she yet alive! He was informed that his loved and sacred mother had departed this life sixteen years ago. Yes, my reader, his mother had been dead sixteen years, and this was his first news of the mournful tidings. How his mother's likeness now sprang up before him; in his imagination, he could recall her parting blessings to her wandering, fortune-seeking son. He now thought of all his early associates, and he consequently had a thousand questions to ask about his old home, and was surprised to hear how many of them were numbered with the dead, and that still many others had moved away; some few like himself had gone no one knew whither; perhaps some of them had shared the same fate as his mountain friend White Cotton.

Eighteen years brings a great change in a neighborhood; had Aleck now returned home, he would have found himself a stranger in his own home. The timber where he had first learned to shoot a rifle while hunting deer, coons, squirrels, etc., was all cleared away, and instead of trees, corn, wheat, potatoes, etc., was now growing. Eighteen years of improvement leaves its mark anywhere, particularly in so rich and fertile a tract of country as St. Clair County, Illinois.

Alexander and his nephews had an interesting time at the Fort, but it was war times now, and all on the move, so many an expected pleasant chat had to be dispensed with; besides, Hughes and Moore shortly after this returned home. They informed their relatives and friends in Illinois that they had found their uncle Cyrus at Fort Sonoma in California, that he was alive and well, had a family, owned a large ranch, and was doing well. Aleck's friends were surprised to hear from him. It was a long while not to hear from a trapper.

But in those days it was nothing new not to hear from the wanderers who left their homes for the Pacific Coast for years at a time. The trappers and hunters knew that great changes were constantly taking place in the states, and as they could not at times send word for years, they would not send word at all, thinking that their friends had removed elsewhere. From this time nothing more was heard from Aleck until July 1850, when the author, Charles Alexander, another nephew of his, ran across him in the Russian River country.[4]

Charles Alexander concluded to remain a while with Cyrus and engage in Agricultural and Stock Raising pursuits, which he did for three years, and up to the present time, has resided within a few miles of his uncle's house. Many a wild and romantic story did Aleck relate to his nephew, also many a dangerous exploit and hair breadth escape from the Indians. As Aleck had been among the Indians twenty years, he knew them if anybody did. The stories that have been and will now be presented are not mere fiction but realities. We would have dated many more of them, but will first explain Aleck's method of keeping time.

[4] See note to Preface.

Residence of Cyrus & Rufina Alexander

Cyrus Alexander

The Mountaineers, in place of an Almanac, kept a stick which they notched, but as they would frequently lose this, they would start another from memory. For this reason, we did not dare to date uncertainties.

Aleck, after remaining at the Fort some time, concluded he would go and take a look at his ranch and see how things looked out there. He left his family in the Fort. He found his ranch in need of repair, and the Indians somewhat pacified. When not needed at the Fort, he would be out on his ranch, leaving his wife and children at the Fort until the war should be over.

We will now give the reader an idea of the struggle for freedom, and some few notes about American California, as Upper California was then called–Catholic California would have been a more appropriate name. American California was discovered by Sir Francis Drake, who was sent out by the English. The English however lost their right of discovery as they sent out no colonies. The Spanish next turned their attention to it. The first permanent settlement in American California was by a Franciscan Mission at San Diego. The Spanish king gave the priests permission to settle the country for the purpose of converting the natives to Christianity. They therefore selected the most fertile valleys, and founded twenty-one Missions, each containing fifteen miles square.

The buildings were all contained in an enclosure made of adobe, to protect the inmates from the natives. As an increase of population was desirable, the

Missions were composed of monks and nuns, the soldiers not being allowed to bring their wives with them. A few however disregarded this order and brought their families with them; hence a few towns sprang up, the largest being Los Angeles, San Diego and San Francisco; the latter was formerly called "Yerba Buena," Yerba meaning *weed*, and Buena meaning *good*. This weed Yerba Buena grew in that vicinity in great quantities; it was and is still used by the Mexicans, Spanish, and Indians for its medicinal qualities.

California while under the Spanish rule constituted part of the viceroyalty of Mexico. When Mexico became a republic, she established a Territorial Government over California with Los Angeles and Monterey as the Headquarters. The most prominent man in California in those days was Capt. Sutter, so often referred to in this work. Sutter was a Swiss by birth, and came here from St. Louis, Missouri. Sutter obtained a grant of land from Mexico containing thirty Spanish leagues square. He located his residence within this, near where the American River flows into the Sacramento River, and near what is now the capital of the state, Sacramento City. Sutter is still living, and is now a beggar supported by the Government, which pays him $2500 per year. Had Sutter been what he ought to have been, he could today have owned California.[5]

Captain Wilkes, one of the early explorers, reported

[5] At the time of the writing of this account, Sutter was living in the Moravian village of Lititz, Lancaster County, Pennsylvania, where he

well of the soil and productions of California.[6] He also stated where the scale was turned in favor of freedom by twenty-five American hunters. Fremont, another early explorer, discovered the South Pass in the Rocky Mountains, the Gateway between the Pacific and Atlantic Coast. He also explored many parts of the country. He and his party stopped to rest and recruit at Sutter's Fort, at the affluent of the American River. Little did Fremont think of the golden treasures under his feet.

Fremont discovered and named many of the rivers, mountain passes, etc., he had the renowned Kit Carson for a guide. Points of interest between 1844 and 1848. In 1844, when Polk became president of the United States he had war upon his hands. His object was to obtain California and New Mexico if possible. But a project was now on foot to place California beyond the reach of the American Government, and place it in the hands of the English. Macnamara,[7] an Irish priest, was to figure conspicuously in this. He

moved after his homestead had been destroyed by fire in 1865. He had been granted in 1864, by act of the California legislature, a monthly pension of $250. Charles Alexander's unsympathetic judgment of Sutter is similar to Bancroft's extremely critical attitude. (Bancroft R-Z, p. 739.)

[6] Captain Charles Wilkes (1798-1877). *Narrative of the United States Exploring Expedition* (5 vols., Philadelphia, 1844).

[7] In 1846, Father Eugene McNamara, a young Irish priest, planned to set up a colony of several thousand Irish Catholics in California, to counteract "further usurpations on the part of an irreligious and anti-Catholic nation." Governor Pico granted him a large tract of land for that purpose, lying in the San Joaquin Valley. (Caughey, *California*, pp. 224-25.)

went to the City of Mexico and obtained grants of the best portions of California.

Fremont had been called on by the American people to be their leader, and was encouraged by Polk. Fremont had sixty-three (63) followers, mostly such men of steel, who knew no fear, like Kit Carson, and furnished with artillery, and armed with Colt's six-shooters. Mr. Polk's intention was to counterwork the British plot, and his agents were well chosen and his plans successful. Polk was afterwards bitterly censured for this. "Whether or not, in performing this service, he undertook and executed more than the constitution of the republic allows to the sole executive power, and thus left dangerous precedents, it belongs to the jurist to decide."

Fremont was afterwards arrested for his part of the contest by General Kearney, who threatened to send him to Washington for trial, but he was afterwards released.[8] The result of the struggle was that California was added to the Union in 1848. The question now arose, would people enough immigrate here to settle up the country? But a way was soon opened, an attraction soon presented itself. *Gold* was discovered, but we will speak of that soon. As to Polk and Fremont, it matters not now what the public thinks of their part, as they meant it all for our country's good; we

[8] Fremont was found guilty by a court martial, held in Washington in 1847-1848, of mutiny, disobedience, and conduct prejudicial to order. Though pardoned by President Polk, he resigned from the service. (Bancroft F-H, pp. 748-49.)

ought to lean on mercy's side in judging of their actions in this struggle. Here the saying is good: "All's well that ends well."

The Revolution now being over, all things again became quiet. The Mexicans and Spanish saw it was best for them to be on friendly terms with the Americans. The Americans have often been tried with similar results. It seems to be a settled fact—"that Americans will rule America." They are a liberal and generous people, but it will not do to try and trample on what they consider their rights. They are very jealous of what they consider *Just Laws* and *Equal Rights*. They will bear oppression for awhile, but it will never do to goad them.

Alexander's friends, the Diggers, thought the best thing they could do was to keep cool. These Diggers had been led into it by the Mexicans, and were glad to keep peace. At best, the California Indians do not possess common Indian sense; they are easily led astray. They care but little for the Mexicans or Americans either, so long as they have enough to eat.

Alexander now employed a gang of Diggers to make adobe for him to continue his house. This building is 80 feet long, 20 feet wide, 12 feet high, and the walls are two feet thick, all of solid adobe. This he called the foundation of his future house; he covered it with a temporary roof to protect the adobe. He now felt satisfied that all the improvements he put on the place would stay there. So he went to work in putting up all the improvements he could.

CHAPTER VI.

The Discovery of Gold in California

CALIFORNIA by this time, 1848, began to attract the attention of the people of the Eastern states. Capt. Wilkes and Capt. Fremont, two of the early explorers, gave flattering reports of the soil, climate, streams, valleys, mountains, etc. Wilkes said the harbor of San Francisco was the finest, if not one of the best in the world. Fremont had discovered and explored a route through the South Pass by which immigrants could immigrate from the states to the Pacific Coast.

A great many people now began to leave their homes and strike out for the "Far West." As an increase of population naturally makes an increase in business, Capt. Sutter erected a sawmill at the junction of the American river. This mill for ever settled the fate of California, for one morning as Mr. Marshall, a hired man, was working in the race-way, he discovered what proved to be gold.[1] This was in the month of February 1848.[2]

It has often been stated that men will fight, starve, and sacrifice their all for their country's sake. They will fight for their homes and fire-sides. But they will do all this, and even much more for gold. Yes; what will man not do for gold? This rumor not only spread over the United States, but over Europe, Asia, South America, and even the islands of the ocean.

The principal rush was made in 1849. All came here with but one thing in view, that of getting rich. Gold was soon afterwards discovered in different localities. Gov. Mason–Military Governor–[3] stated in a letter to the President as follows: "As I passed along, I found houses deserted, fields of wheat going to ruin, their owners having left them to dig for Gold. I followed up the American river to the saw-mill, in whose raceway the golden scales were first discovered. I visited the *Placers*, and saw multitudes engaged in the beds of streams, and in dry ravines, where water courses had once existed. In a little gutter, two men had found the value of $17,000."

Gold had been found in such quantities that every

[1]James W. Marshall (1810-1885) who came to California in the Clyman emigrant party in 1845, erected the sawmill for Sutter on the south fork of the American River at what is now Coloma, about forty miles northeast of Sacramento.

[2] The date was January 24, 1848.

[3] Richard Barnes Mason (1797-1850) was military governor of California from 1847 to 1849.

convenience of life bore an enormous price. Capt. Sutter paid his blacksmith $10 per day, and he received $500 per month rent for a two story house within his Fort. The average yield for a day's labor was two ounces, and an ounce was then worth or valued at $16. California at once became the center of attraction; all eyes were turned toward the Golden State. There was a rush for the Gold Fields.

The territory was uncultivated at the time, and the result was starvation for many; they now began to murder and steal. The mines were crowded; thousands were gathering from every land, attracted by the sovereign power of gold. Mason was Military Governor; he and the people soon found it necessary to enact a very strict law. At first it was informal, and any one found guilty of high crimes was hung without delay or ceremony. Thus many a gold seeker got more than he bargained for.

It was almost beyond belief how California began to settle up. It was now a large territory with here and there a stock-raiser, and now and then a wheat grower. Now the valleys were overrun with miners; strange ships sailed in the Bays, rivers were navigated, and towns sprang up like enchantment. No country in the world ever became so widely known and popular in so short a space of time, or received such a tide of immigrants. People of every race, color, language, character, occupation and nationality in the world, all aiming at the one thing, gold.

Rufina Alexander

ALEXANDER CHILDREN: *Margaret, Thomas, George Cyrus, and Caroline*

The largest amount mined in one year was in 1843.[4] $65,000,000 were taken from the mines that year. $1,000,000,000 have been taken from the mines since 1849. And there still seems to be gold in abundance in the Sierra Nevada Mountain Range, in the eastern part of the state. As it was impossible for the mines to give employment to all, they began to scatter throughout the Coast, into the valleys, mountains, also into Oregon, in search of homes, some seeking stock ranches, others farming ground; any where, any thing to get rich.

Fortune did not smile on all. Some turned out *hard cases*; perhaps the scum of civilization came here; gambling became universal, and is still followed to a great extent in the Golden State and adjoining states and territories. Provision was very scarce, and many an unlucky miner bitterly regretted the day he left his home to get rich in the gold mines of California. Today many are rushing to the Black Hills with the same object in view.

The people beginning to settle here and the rush to the mines proved a good thing for Alexander. It created a market for his stock, fruit, vegetables, etc., and brought the long sought for money to his coffers. He slaughtered no more cattle merely for their hides and tallow; he could do much better with them now;

[4] This is obviously an error. According to Rodman W. Paul, in *California Gold*, p. 345, fiscal year 1852 showed the highest value of gold produced in California: $81,294,700. The figure for 1853 is $67,613,487.

he drove them to the mines and received almost fabulous prices for them there. Drovers came to the ranch for them, paying good prices, all in gold dust, and saving Aleck the trouble of driving them to the mines.

He also owned some sheep, but the wolves and coyotes had made so many raids upon them that the band had not increased very much. As it required a great deal of time and trouble to take care of them, he sold them to the drovers, and received sixteen dollars per head for them, the drover's own offer. After selling his sheep, he found that the wolves and other wild animals were killing his calves. As stock was worth money now, he thought he would put a stop to their depredations, also to try and get his cattle gentle, as it was now necessary to drive them up more than once a year, as he had done heretofore.

He now picked out some of the best cows and heifers, and corraled them, with the intention of milking them and teaching them what *so!* meant. Some of them would not *so!* worth a cent. It was quite a ludicrous affair to see how this training and milking operation was performed. After selecting the animal to be performed upon–he caught them with that indispensable thing, the lariat–she then had her head drawn down to the fence; during this time she would rear, kick, plunge, jump, and use her horns freely, and try every way imaginable to gain her freedom. This however was only fun for the boys; they now took a strap with a running loop at one end; with this they would fasten her hind legs together, and then they tied the strap to her tail; after this she could be milked without any more ceremony. After a few repetitions of the above management, and by being careful, the cows would become gentle, and some of them would turn out good milkers, and bring big prices at the mines.

We never learned where Aleck got his first hogs, but when we met him in 1850, he had quite a drove of fine hogs, all of them very large, and as white and nice as hogs generally get. These hogs kept in a good condition on the wild clover, and were trained to come home at night by having a light "feed" of wheat. Aleck was the only person in this section of the country that owned hogs, and they were worth a great deal of money. In the fall of the year 1850, he had twenty head of fine stock hogs, very nice and fat, and weighing perhaps from three to four hundred pounds apiece.

A drover by the name of Olmstead came along from the mines one day, and after stating that he wished to purchase the hogs, asked Aleck how much he would take for them. Aleck replied that he would take $50 apiece for the hogs. Olmstead had been a wheat grower in Illinois, and professed to understand all he was about in all his business transactions. He thought he could manage to get the hogs for less than the price named. But Aleck meant what he said, and would not change his price.

Olmstead wanted to know how much that would

be per pound, but they had nothing to weigh them with. Olmstead at last hit upon a novel plan. He asked if there was any wheat on the ranch, and after being informed that there was, he said: "Put a rail through the fence, and fasten a hog on one end and a sack of wheat on the other, and see if it will balance." Aleck asked him how he would know how much the wheat would weigh. "Oh," said Olmstead, "I can guess at that. Mr. Alexander replied, why not guess at the weight of the hog in the first place then! But this was not so certain a matter for the drover; he had been a wheat grower and was pretty well posted in the weight of wheat, but knew nothing about the weight of hogs. The chances are that the drover would have lost by the operation in the end, as it would have taken more than one sack of wheat to poise the hog; besides, wheat weighs much heavier to the sack in California than it does in Illinois. Suffice it to say that the drover took the hogs and paid $50 apiece for them. $1000 is a big price to pay for twenty stock hogs, but hogs in those days were not so numerous in California as they are today.

Every thing sold at this rate proportionally. The people, after crossing the plains, were nearly all attacked with the scurvy, caused by salted meat. They now craved for fresh meat and vegetables; besides this, they must have something to eat, and every thing in that line was scarce.

Aleck now thought he would make a raid upon the

wild animals and clean them out, if possible. His stock was now too valuable to feed to the wild animals. He sent to San Francisco and procured some *nux vomica*, a rank poison; this he broke up into small pieces, and put them into water, and boiled; in this decoction, he soaked slices of meat, and dragged the meat in such a manner as to make a trail across the animals' path, and then dropped the poisoned meat in the trail so that the animal would be sure to find it. In the morning all the animals that had been unfortunate enough to eat the poisoned meat would be found dead near the spot where the meat lay.

Some times he would succeed in killing half a dozen in one night. He also caught many in traps; if there was one thing in which Alexander excelled it was in the skill of handling traps. He had been a trapper so long that trapping seemed to be a second nature to him. He knew just how, when, and where to set a trap, and what to bait it with, and the different seasons and stages of weather for trapping. After a season of poisoning and trapping, his stock would have peace for a while at least.

Poisoning wild animals is much resorted to yet in California. The large wild animals are mostly killed off. And the Ground-squirrels, Jack-rabbits, Skunks, Civet-Cats, and numerous other animals and vermin trouble the grain and poultry. The Ground-squirrel and Jack-rabbit in particular are great pests. The Ground-squirrels burrow in hill-sides among the rocks and are hard to exterminate. Many are caught and killed in steel traps.

As California was now settling up fast, and the people must be governed by a Constitutional law, they now clamored to be admitted into the Union as a state. The principal difficulty was, should she be admitted as a free or as a slave state? President Taylor gave the Californians the timely assurance that "Whatever can be done to afford the people of the Territories the benefits of Civil government and the protection that is due them will be anxiously considered and attempted by the executive." He also suggested to them the expediency of forming for themselves a state government thereafter to be submitted to congress. General Riley, who succeeded Mason as military governor, issued a proclamation inviting the citizens to choose delegates to form a state constitution. The delegates met at Monterey September 1st, 1849. The constitution they formed was accepted by the people.[5] Slavery had in the meantime been decided against by a special convention which had been held at San Francisco. The first Legislature met at San Jose December 20th, 1849. The choice of representatives to congress fell upon J. C. Fremont and W. M. Gwin,[6] who carried the constitution of California to Washington.

[5] General Bennett Riley (1787-1853) was military governor of California from April to December 1849. In September of that year he convened the constitutional assembly at Monterey, which drew up the first California Constitution and applied for admission into the union. General Riley was succeeded on December 20 by Peter Burnett, the first civil governor.

[6] William McKendree Gwin (1805-1885).

The clause striking out slavery caused a bitter debate by the Southern members in Congress, and aided to bring on Clay's renowned Compromise Bill. On the 7th of September, 1850, California was admitted, with her boundaries extending from Oregon to the Mexican Possessions. Alexander was in favor of the clause striking out slavery, and used his influence among the Mexicans, as well as among the Americans. The first election Aleck attended was held at the house of Mr. Campbell, two miles southwest from where the little one-horse-town of Windsor now stands.

Aleck now went to work to raise vegetables for the mines, and in the summer of 1850 succeeded in raising a good crop of extra and large onions. This was his first attempt, and he raised about two tons; it encouraged him. He sent these to the mines in an ox team, and cleared about $1200 in gold dust. He retailed the onions at from 40 to 75 cents per pound. As the valleys were now filling up, they began to select names for the different localities. Alexander's Ranch was called Alexander Valley; Santa Rosa Ranch was named Santa Rosa—a fine and flourishing town, the county seat of Sonoma County now stands here. Mark West's Ranch is divided into numerous farms and several stations. 1st, Mark West Station on the Donahue R. R., 2nd, Old Mark West, 3rd, Mark West Springs. Besides these, there are many other names, as Russian River, Bodega, Knight's Valley, Dry Creek Valley, Poor Man's Flat, etc.

Aleck's apple and peach trees had now grown up to be trees; his grapes had also flourished, and all were now bearing well, showing that California was a good fruit growing country. Aleck now had more fruit than he could use in his family. The pioneer settlers were a jovial fun-loving people, full of fun and fond of fruit; a crowd would collect at Alexander's during the fruit season, and all have a good time. During this season of the year, all would have leisure time, as there was then not much work on hand. California Farmers do not work the year round in California like they do in most of the states.

The gold excitement now ran higher than ever before; reports reached Aleck of the fortunes made in a few days. Many of the ranchers were deserting their ranches and going to the mines. Aleck was doing well, but like many more, he was not satisfied with well, he thought he could do better. So after making arrangements, he left his ranch under the supervision of his wife and started for the mines.

Arriving at the mines on the American and Sacramento rivers, he found them already over-run. Some good strikes had been made, but the majority had lost what little they had. Alexander worked hard, but Dame Fortune was only coquetting with him; as he had no success, he started for Yuba River; here he worked early and late; some were doing well, but Aleck had no luck. He thought of returning home, but as others were going to the Feather River, he accompanied them there. Here opposition and poor luck followed him in every move he made. He worked and toiled on however until he was taken with the Chills and Fever. This settled his fate as a gold miner; he had had experience with the Chills and Fever in Illinois in his boyhood days and knew what it was.

He was now satisfied that his fortune did not lay in the mines and concluded to abandon them forever. He had tried lead mining to his satisfaction in Illinois, and now gold mining did not seem to pay any better. So he sold his tools and started for home, his mind now fully made up to stick to his ranch, and never more attempt to get rich quickly. How many have learned that there is more wealth within a foot of the soil than in all the gold mines.

Arriving at home, Aleck concluded to stick to his ranch; he knew this would pay in the long run if he would only have patience. He enjoyed good health, and had many a gay time at his ranch. The people who would call on him during the fruit season managed to keep things lively; during the day-time, the company would amuse themselves in various ways, and at night they would have a dance. They somehow always managed to have a fiddler with them who could make "Old Dan Tucker" hum in California as well as elsewhere. Aleck had a good floor in his large house, and many a young gallant "honored his partner" upon it.

One thing we will mention here about Alexander.

From this time up he did not keep whiskey in his house; consequently his friends did not get tipsy, and they always contrived to have a good time; this proves that people can have a good time at a dance without whiskey if they so make up their minds. Many a Party has been spoiled and many a warm friendship blighted by having intoxicating liquor at parties. Harm can be made out of anything, particularly when there is liquor on hand.[7]

About this time, 1851, Aleck had occasion to remodel part of his house; when he came to his wheat bin, he found the wheat next to the wall had heated and was musky and spoiled, and part of it was alive with the black weevil. It was damaged for seed wheat, or flour either; some of the unbolted flour on hand was in a similar condition. It looked like a pity to waste it, but what could he do with it? Wheat was now very high, as all that could be raised was shipped to the mines. But an unexpected market opened for the weevil eaten and damaged wheat and flour. An old man named Miller had crossed the plains a few years previous, bringing with him some of the machinery for a Distillery. He had heard of the said wheat, and thought it would do to make whiskey. So far, Miller had been unable to get any thing to feed his still with, so he went to see Aleck and see what he

[7] "Cyrus Alexander was revolutionary in his time because he did not have whiskey at his dances in the early 1850's, maintaining that people could have a good time at the dances without a jug." (Hansen and Miller, *Wild Oats in Eden*, p. 116.)

could do about it. If it would make good whiskey, he would be able to make a big thing out of it. Miller took a look at it and concluded it would do. He bargained for it all at ten cents per pound, and packed it up and took it to his distillery.

He had employment now, and besides this, he had a new thing to experiment with; would such stuff make whiskey or not? These were the first and only weevils we have ever seen in this state. Perhaps the distillery will stop propagation; at any rate it stopped propagation here. There is a circumstance connected with this distillery too good to be lost. Miller and his wife Aunt Katie were both very fond of liquor. And as it was a very difficult matter always to get material to manufacture it of, the grain being scarce and high, whiskey even at the Still would get scarce. At one time the men folks were all going from home to celebrate the 4th of July and have a big spree. They had a jug of whiskey, and it was not convenient to take either the jug or Aunt Katie with them, and it would never do to leave both at home. So one of them, being of an ingenious turn of mind, solved the difficult question as follows. He took the jug and clumb up a tree with it, and tied it far up above the reach of Aunt Katie, and then they went away, satisfied with their plan, and thinking they had "got away with the old woman that time." But time will tell. After the men had been gone some time, Aunt Katie began to long for her usual dram, and she was determined to have it. When a woman once makes up her mind to have a thing, she will have it, let the consequences be what they will. And such was the case with Aunt Katie. She began prospecting for the jug, and at last discovered it up in the tree, but was at a loss how to tackle it. She knew why it had been placed there, and was now more determined than ever to smell of its contents. She pondered awhile, and hit upon a strange plan for a woman, but a good one to gain her point.

She carried out a large wash-tub, and taking the bearings, placed it under the jug, and then, getting her husband's rifle, she went for the jug as if it had been a panther. She took good aim and "blazed away," and sent a bullet whistling through the jug. Out came the longed for "inspiration" in a continual flow. Aunt Katie now had all the 4th of July and independence she wished. She rallied around the tub all day, and was not far from the tub when the men returned. The men, on seeing how things had turned out, took a good laugh and concluded that Aunt Katie was one ahead of them.

Aleck now began to build a large barn. He was now enabled to get sawed lumber at a saw-mill on Mill creek. Lumber was very high, and he employed a carpenter to help put up the building. After finishing this, he concluded to use some more lumber on his house, and made arrangements with the owners of the mill, March and Heald, to exchange pigs for lumber. Common lumber then was worth seventy-five dollars per thousand feet. And a gilt pig was worth seventy-five dollars. So it was an even exchange, a pig for a thousand feet of lumber. After using about ten thousand feet of lumber, his carpenter informed him that he would have to have some more lumber. Aleck replied: "That will take another pig."

CHAPTER VII.

Aleck Troubled with his Land

THE LAND question was now being considerably agitated. As this business is one of the curses of every new state, it can not be expected that California should be an exception. This same neighborhood has similar brawls on hand, even at the time of writing. The United States Land Commissioners were now busy at work, confirming such of the Spanish titles and grants as were brought before them.

Some of the immigrants coming to the Russian River Valley were highly pleased with the Alexander Valley, and thinking that they knew all about the land laws, came to the conclusion that Aleck had more land than he could hold under the new state law. Also that the chances were that the Sotoyome Grant might not be confirmed. They now began to annoy and trouble Aleck by squatting on different portions of his extensive ranch. Aleck, understanding his business and knowing what class of men he had to deal with, never stopped to quarrel with them. He would merely warn the squatters to pull up their stakes and leave. If they did not take his advice, he would coolly inform them what the consequences would be if they did not leave at a certain time. This as a general thing would result in a quiet leave taking, Aleck paying them a fair price for the rails and improvements.

Alexander, finding that the people really wanted his land and that some were willing to pay for it, concluded to dispose of his wild cattle, get a surveyor to survey his land, and then, after making two reserves, he offered the remainder for sale in lots to suit purchasers. Alexander Valley soon began to settle up now. Its inhabitants are mostly from Illinois, Iowa, Tennessee, Missouri, Indiana, and New York.

There were now, 1852, a number of different settlements; they naturally began to attract the attention of Pioneer Preachers. It must be true that teachers, preachers, and civilization go together. The Methodist Conference now sent a man to minister to and look after the spiritual wants of the people of this vicinity. The man sent was Rev. A. L. S. Bateman from Ohio, who is still in the Conference. His circuit then included all the country from Petaluma to Big River, distant about one hundred and fifty miles. Some may think this a big circuit, but in those days California preachers did not sport plug hats and ride around in top-buggies as they do today, but were compelled to ride horse or mule back, and when the streams were swollen, they had to swim them, oftentimes beside their horses.

It was Rev. Bateman's business to hunt up the people and preach the gospel to them. Many of the early settlers had not heard the gospel preached for years, some of them not since they had been boys. Bateman soon found his way into Alexander Valley, and finding several Methodist families here, he was encouraged to make this Valley one of his stopping places. Alexander voluntarily offered his best room in the house as a place for worship.

Reading matter had been very scarce up to this time; books were very scarce and newspapers almost unknown in this section of the Union. In this year, 1852, the author's wife came here from St. Clair County, Illinois. She brought her Bible with her, and one Sunday afternoon, after she had been reading a chapter, she laid the Bible on the table and went out to take a walk. On returning to the house she found that Aleck had been reading in the book, as he made the remark: "That is curious reading; I wonder if it is true!"

It had been a long while since Alexander had read the Bible. Twenty-two years had passed over his head since he had perused its sacred pages; no wonder that he thought it was "curious reading." In reading and education, fate seemed to be against our hero. When his father settled in Illinois, schools were almost unknown, and he grew to man's estate without the many educational advantages that the boys now enjoy. After arriving at manhood, he left his home, and for twenty-two years, he lived without books, schools, or churches. It is a wonder that he did not forget to read entirely. Twenty-two years is a long while to deteriorate in.

Alex, properly speaking, hardly knew what an enlightened country was. He had never lived in a neighborhood where civilization showed in its best light. It is true, the last few years of his life, he had good and enlightened neighbors, but he was then failing in health and strength, and did not enjoy their society as he would have done had they been with him at an earlier time of life.

Aleck now became interested in his Bible, and soon after, having occasion to go to "Frisco," on his return he brought a Bible with him, with large print. This furnished him reading matter for some time; it reminded him of his youth; it brought his Mother's training to his mind. He now saw why she had taught him to lisp "Our Father who art in heaven." How many of the rising generation neglect and pass too slightly over these important things.

From this time on, Aleck's house was furnished with such books and papers as he could then obtain. He knew what it was to live without books, and he now knew how to appreciate and enjoy them. The same minister, Bateman, was sent back the next year with the instructions of building a church if possible. He selected Alexander Valley as a suitable place, and with the very liberal help from Aleck and the people in the Valley, he succeeded in building a small house to be used in worshiping God.

A Sunday School was soon organized in this same building, Aleck and his family attending regularly. This was the first and so far the only church built in this Valley. This church was burned down about ten years afterwards by a supposed incendiary, as it is said that the "Devil always has work for idle hands to do." Perhaps he employed some one to apply the match to the building.

A day school had been kept in this house for some time, but finding that it was not central enough to accommodate the people, Aleck built a School House on his own land, and at his own expense, and offered it to his neighbors for their special benefit. He assisted them to employ teachers, and helped to maintain the school. And during vacation he employed private teachers for his family. This School House, now called "Pine Grove," is still standing, and is used as a School House during the week days and a church Sundays. All denominations preach here.

As Bateman could not come oftener than once in two weeks, Aleck made arrangements with Rev. James Woods[1] to preach at the School House. And to induce him to settle in the neighborhood, and with the aid of his boys help to sustain a school, Aleck presented him a very nice farm, with good soil. You will

[1] See *Recollections of Pioneer Work in California*, by Rev. James A. Woods, pp. 214-19.

see by this that Mr. Woods had better luck than the average run of preachers. It will also be seen that Mr. Alexander became suddenly interested in Education and Religion in 1852.

We have before spoken of the two reserves he made when he decided to sell his land in lots to suit purchasers; perhaps we had better call one of them a homestead. The reserve contains six hundred acres; this he fenced and farmed by renters; it is still farmed in that way. He tired of tramping out his grain with horses; this was too slow and tedious for him. So he purchased a threshing machine of the endless-chain, tread power patent. Do not know as we ought to call this a regular threshing-machine, as it did not separate the grain from the chaff; instead of a separator he had a winnower. He also purchased a fan-mill; this he used in connection with his thresher. He now bought grain-cradles and cradled his grain instead of using sickles. Mr. Alexander threshed his own grain and threshed the grain of his neighbors also; this was in 1853.

As it was the object of Aleck to have the pioneer orchard of the valley, he wanted this orchard to contain the best variety of fruit extant. He spared neither time nor money in trying to carry out his plans. By inquiry he found that a man in Napa Valley had a few more trees than he wanted, and that he would sell them at a dollar apiece. Aleck immediately engaged them, and when it was time to set them out, he went down to Napa Valley to get them. Aleck and the man went to the Nursery to get them; mark their surprise when they discovered that the trees had already been transplanted. Aleck was evidently not the only man who wanted a pioneer orchard; some one had bought the trees when the owner was not at home. The owner never found out who had borrowed the trees. This was quite a disappointment to Aleck, as he was now compelled to wait another year for his trees. The trees he had planted in 1846 were thriving and doing well. He was now satisfied that California would make a fruit growing country, and was very anxious to enlarge his orchard, but as he could obtain no trees, he had to wait until the Spring of 1854 before he would have a chance to procure any more trees.

Aleck now prospered as well as he could wish; everything went lovely until the spring of 1856, when the Squatters began to molest him again. His land was a fertile tract, and drew the attention of every one who chanced to come that way. All considered him a "Land-grabber," they could not understand how he could honestly own so large a tract of land; they did not stop to think that it was a "Spanish Claim" and that he lived upon it before California was a state, even before it was a Territory, and still further back, he lived upon it long before California belonged to the United States. One unprincipled, unreasonable, and dare-devil family took up their residence in the center of his wheat fields on "the Reserve." He made himself at home here, and had the audacity and meanness to turn his stock at large into the grain fields. There are many very mean men in this country, but this one must have been one of the first water. Aleck went to see this man and warned him off; according to law, this was all he could do in the case.

The squatter paid no attention to this, but went on with his depredations. Aleck left him remain until Fall, and after he had gathered his crops, he called on the County Sheriff to assist him in getting rid of the squatter. The sheriff informed the squatter that he was trespassing and that he was aware that the land was the property of another; that the best thing he could do was to pack up his traps and leave; that if he did not leave, he–the sheriff–would be compelled to use his authority and move him against his will.

The squatter paid no attention to the sheriff's threat, so the sheriff came to the neighborhood, summoned his posse, and telling all to be ready for action in the morning, he again informed the squatter of his intentions. That night Alexander's barn was burned with all its contents. The barn at the time contained his crop of grain just threshed, his threshing machine, fan-mill, plows, grain cradles, rakes, and various other farming utensils; a rick of grain near the barn was also consumed. All that Aleck could do towards saving anything was to remove his fence and save some of the rails, and turn out his horses. He did this with his eyes open and his trusty rifle in his right hand.

The next morning the squatter was gone. It did not take a Philadelphia lawyer to tell who had applied the match to the barn. This fire was a great loss to Aleck; the barn was a valuable building; he also lost his last year's crop; he was now out of bread for a year to come; he also had to buy his seed wheat. The fire was also a loss to the neighborhood, as it burned the first and only threshing-machine in this part of the country. Although Aleck felt his great loss, he was never heard to complain or make any revengeful threats against any one, but went on quietly with his business as if nothing had happened.

Aleck had always been molested by wild animals, but now a huge Grizzly began to make raids upon them. This bear was in the habit of helping himself to pork whenever His Majesty's wishes inclined that way. Aleck had tried various means to capture or kill this animal, but had not been successful. The "old fellow" killed a large fat hog one night and left about half of it on the spot where he had killed it under a large live oak tree. Aleck, the author, and another man now concluded to capture this animal.

They knew he would be back again the next night, to get the meat he had left or to get another pig. So they drove all the hogs they could find into a pen, and when they had quieted down, they left a gap in the bars, so that the stragglers could come in, should any of them be out. They then stationed themselves, gun in hand, so that they could watch both the pen and the remains of the hog. The night was very dark and rainy, just the night for old bruin to prowl around in to search for grub.

They had been stationed on their beat about three hours when they heard the pigs squeal in the pen near the house. They now ran for the house and found old bruin at work on the pigs; the bear had stationed himself at the bars, and as fast as a pig would approach, he would slap him over with his paw; he had killed two outright, and had torn and mangled several others at a fearful rate. The old veteran had found out that if he would frighten the pigs, they would try and get out of the pen; for this reason he watched the gap. As the men neared the pen, the bear took to the mountains, and none of them got a chance for a fair shot at him; it did not pay to fool with Grizzlies or to risk a poor shot. Aleck was now determined to capture the old veteran, as it did not pay to have him around; pork was too scarce and valuable for bear grub.

Aleck now went to work to build a log cabin bear trap; it was about eight feet by ten; it took several hard days' work to finish it. They then dug a hole, and put a log floor into it upon which a trap was to rest. The corners of the trap were notched and primed in such a manner that the logs did not have any loop holes for the bear to get his paws through. Aleck then went to work to contrive a large and strong trap door, but not getting it finished the first evening, they put some meat into the trap to lure the bear into it. He came, took the meat, and went back into the mountains. This just suited Aleck; the next day he finished the door, and baited the trap with pig. He arranged this door upon a double trigger plan, similar to the "Box-skunk traps" of today. It worked admirably.

The next morning early, when Aleck went to look at his trap, he found the door down, and the trap occupied by the bear. Aleck was so elated with his success, that he went back to the house and called his fellow hunters, also his wife and children, to come and look at the bear. The old fellow did not enjoy his situation a bit, and was very cross–but then it was enough to make anybody mad; perhaps the bear, like Patrick Henry, wanted Liberty or death. Aleck and his two pards each enjoyed two shots apiece at the "poor fellow," who made a fearful noise at the first few shots, but soon cooled down.

After they thought the bear was dead, Aleck very cautiously opened the door and said."Look out now," but his caution was unnecessary. The pig-eater was dead. He was a very large animal, one of the largest of his species that Aleck had ever seen, and he had killed many bears. They put him down at nine hundred pounds. Do not know how they weighed him; perhaps the same way that Olmstead wanted to weigh the hogs. They could not load him on the wagon, so

Aleck fixed some slides, and hitched his oxen to him and dragged him on the wagon in that way.

The next thing we find our hero engaged in was trying to get ahead of a panther. These animals were very troublesome among colts, calves, hogs, etc. One morning he heard the pigs which nested near the house squealing, the dogs were barking, and there evidently was some excitement on hand. He jumped up and started towards the pigpen, and found a large panther who had just picked up the old sow and was on his way to the mountains with her. He had left the pigs undisturbed. Aleck followed him cautiously up a branch, or ravine, and saw him stop. Aleck then returned to the house for his gun.

He now went back to the place where he last saw he panther, but on arriving at the spot, he foundt the panther had *vamosed.* The panther had killed the old sow, and then dragged her into the brush and buried her. Aleck felt satisfied that he could get away with him when he returned for the sow—panthers always come back when they bury their plunder. So he hunted up and prepared his steel trap, but fearing it would be too weak, he put another trap near the first in hopes he would tread into both at the same time. He set his traps near the hog in the brush and waited to see what the result would be. The first night, the panther returned and eat part of the hog, and got his paw into the weakest trap, but succeeded in getting away. He returned again the next night and had the misfortune of getting into both traps at the same time, so he now concluded to remain until morning, when Aleck came and gave him a dose of "blue-pill" which ended his career as a "pork packer." This panther was a very large animal, about the size of a large deer, and his skin was as large as that of a yearling calf.

These incidents are here mentioned to give some of our young readers an idea of what men in a new country have to contend with; California was not always the fine improved country that it is today. Pioneers have much to put up with, many hardships to endure; they do not have everything at their command as they have in old settled countries. But the wild animals of California are fast disappearing before the march of civilization. After the country settled up. Aleck and his neighbors hunted until they had thinned out the most in their vicinity. Panthers, coyotes, have not been seen for years; sometimes, but very seldom, a bear is killed; deer are still hunted and many are killed, but in a few years more, even the deer will have passed away. The renowned Jack-rabbits are still to be found, but in many parts are getting wild and shy.

When Aleck divided up his land, he put his wild cattle on shares. Stock such as sheep and Angora goats are still raised here in this manner; men owning hundreds of acres of foothill land take sheep or goats, or some times both, on shares, for one, two, or three years; they herd them on the hills. The man grazing the sheep gets one half of the increase of the flock and half of the wool. It does not require much money to start in the stock, and both parties generally make it pay well. Sometimes men *bust* at it, but then men are apt to *bust* at anything.

Quite a number of people having settled in this vicinity, they found it convenient to have a store nearer than Santa Rosa. An enterprising settler named Harmon Heald volunteered to embark in this business. He selected for his building site a place near the Sawmill of March and Heald, and where the flourishing town of Healdsburg now stands.[2] This place soon became the center of operations, and others soon began to settle here, until one trade after another was represented. It was soon to be seen that Healdsburg was going to be a town, as it had a good and healthy location.

The people now began to look up the School and Church matters. We have before stated Alexander's liberality in helping in this line of business at home; he now seemed just as willing to help others. Money always demanded a high rate of interest in California, interest here being computed by the month at the rate of from one to five cents per month. Aleck now volunteered to let the Methodist Society of Healdsburg have enough money to build a church at a low rate of interest. The church was built, and the society being too weak and poor to refund the money, he afterwards purchased the building and paid a fair price

[2] In his *Recollections of Pioneer Work in California*, pp. 214-19, the Rev. James Wood tells of the founding of Healdsburg by Harmon Heald, and of Cyrus Alexander's connections with early Healdsburg.

for it. He did not *grab* the building; he gave them every chance they could wish for before he took the house.

As he had no use for the Church, and as the Presbyterian Society was now organizing at Healdsburg, and he being in sympathy with that order, he presented the church to them. At the time Alexander presented the church to the Presbyterians, he was a member of that church. The church is still standing, and is still under the control of the Presbyterians. Rev. J. Woods was then the pastor of the Presbyterian church; he immediately removed from Santa Rosa to Healdsburg. He now resides in San Francisco, and preached a short time since at Healdsburg in the same "little Brown church round the corner." Alexander always made it an object to help all benevolent societies, no matter what shade or color, and he was ever ready to help all educational enterprises. He knew what it was to be without books and papers.

CHAPTER VIII.

The Civil War

IT OFTEN HAPPENED that some of his land purchasers were not ready with the money when the installments fell due. It made no difference to Aleck; he was ever ready to extend the time and wait until his purchasers had a chance to earn some money. Money in those days demanded a high rate of interest, and Aleck could have made a big thing in demanding the same interest that other wealthy men were drawing on their money. But he thought that 10% per annum was enough. Money was worth from one to five % per month.

Another thing we wish to state about him is this: he was never known to foreclose a mortgage in a hurry, or to crowd a person for money. Alexander had been a poor man, and had worked hard for every dollar he possessed, and he knew how to sympathize with others who were struggling with life's earnest battles. He had many chances and inducements to make money off of others of the poorer classes, but he was too manly to stoop so low.

When the late Civil War broke out and threatened to sunder our Union, Alexander sided with the North. He was in favor of preserving the Union at all hazards. The War caused bitter feelings here as well as elsewhere. Many good men hesitated; should they side with the North or South? The war is over and all bitter enmities caused by it should be forgotten. But in California we have noticed that a bitter feeling still exists; Californians do not look at things in the same light that we do in the Eastern states. Here you can yet hear men howl and talk about the Federal Union, and many that never smelled gun powder during the war howled about the rebels. We hope they will soon look at things in the same light that the inhabitants in the Eastern states do. When the U. S. Bonds were first thrown upon the market for sale, Aleck concluded that he could do his country some service by purchasing bonds. He therefore invested much of his hard earned money in bonds.

Mr. Alexander now felt old age creeping on; he had led a busy life; the hard work and rough usage, camp life, etc., all began to tell on him at last. He now had his ranch improved and fitted up, so he busied himself in overseeing the work, trying new experiments in the agricultural line, etc.; he was now considered a wealthy man; he had acquired what he had so long toiled and struggled for. But little did he think of the sorrow and heart-rendering trials yet in store for him before he would be called to close his earthly career and eventful life by his maker.

His taxes now—just after the war—amounted to from $1500 to $2000 a year, quite an item. Taxes are higher here than in any other state we have ever been in. The Russian River country and Healdsburg now began to improve; it was a good farming country, and immigrants began to pour in. Land now demanded a fair price. Dry Creek Valley near Healdsburg also began to develop itself as a farming country. Healdsburg as a town began to develop and show rapid improvements, and the people began to talk Rail Road. Alexander took a lively interest in all that was going on; he was ever ready to help in any or all improvements, but as the proposed Rail Road was to connect Healdsburg to San Francisco, and did not pass through or near Alexander Valley, he did not think it advisable to take stock in the concern.

Alexander saw that he could help the struggling population by furnishing them money at low rates of interest. This he did cheerfully, he taking mortgages on the property for security, and then leaving his creditors have a chance to get a start. He was very particular about having every thing done in a legal manner; notwithstanding all this he was never known to be severe. But in spite of all his watchfulness and dear experience, he would sometimes get taken in by Sharpers and Shysters.

California has always been a speculating country—Mining stock speculations, Land speculations, Live Stock speculations, and worst of all, "Wild Cat" speculations. Many an honest hard working plodding man has been cheated out of his all by these Sharpers, and their "Wild Cat" speculations. It seems to be understood by many that in California you are either on the top or on the bottom of the ladder, most frequently at the bottom, as speculations like many other things are carried on to extremes.

In one instance, a certain Doctor, a friend of Alexander and a family physician, who had Aleck's entire confidence, and with whom Aleck had always dealt fairly and squarely, and had helped when in need, knowing his influence over Alexander, came to him and told him glowing stories about a new gold discovery and the Washita Mines, and prevailed on Aleck to loan him some money to invest. He represented the mine as a big thing, and offered to give the best of security in improved town property. Aleck "shelled out" several hundred dollars. The mine turned out a "Wild Cat" speculation, and Aleck found out that the town property did not amount to much. The result was Aleck was out several hundred dollars; so much for misplaced confidence. If any one mentioned the affair to Mr. A. and asked him what he thought of his friend, the Doctor, he would reply that he "was a bad egg."

At another time a certain Judge of Sonoma County,

one of the "big guns," represented himself as an agent for a Water Company that was going to supply Virginia City, Nevada, with water-works and an aqueduct that would supply water in abundance. The Judge was selling stock and soliciting help. He represented this as a "big paying thing," stating that none but the best citizens and moneyed men were taking stock, and that he did not care about selling stock to any men but such as Mr. A. He talked long and used honeyed words and flowery language to Mr. A. The result was Mr. A. took four thousand dollars worth of stock. This also turned out a "Wild Cat" speculation, and Mr. A. lost $4000 by the operation. On asking Mr. A. what he thought of the Judge, he replied "that he was a swindler of the smart kind." This is a sample of his remarks about any one; he used as few words as possible, and never censured or seemed to blame any one very much, but took his losses as a matter of course.

With the exception of the "Priest affair," which would raise his temper every time it was mentioned to him, and whom he never forgave, he never spoke ill of any one if he could avoid it. This unjust Judge took the money he had swindled Mr. A. and others out of, and secured a homestead for his wife in San Francisco. He is wealthy now, and blows and brags about his ill-gotten gains. He is still living in Sonoma County, California.

About the 1st of September 1865, Mr. A. was stricken down by Paralysis. The stroke was a severe one, and had he not had the best of Physicians, and patient and never tiring friends and nurses, he would never have survived this shock. He never did recover entirely, but he was enabled to move around some; but it was only with half of the physical man; he had lost the use entirely of half of his body; even half of his tongue refused to fulfill its office. His relatives, friends, associates, and everybody seemed to sympathize with him in this, his great affliction. All saw that an honest, thriving, energetic business man would now be called from the daily routine of business. Alexander had been a leading man in all the ups and downs; now he would be confined to his home, and the inquiry in the valley was—How is Uncle Cyrus—as he was familiarly called. But the worst blow for Aleck was that he would now forever have to give up the long nurtured hope of ever again returning to Illinois to visit his early friends and his relatives. He had watched the Great Union Pacific Rail Road, and expected to ride the Iron Horse across the Mountains and Plains, where he had spent months and years hunting the buffalo, deer, bear, beaver, otter, etc.

He had now been from home thirty-five years, and nothing would have given him more pleasure than to revisit his early stamping ground, where his boyhood days had been spent. St. Louis was a city now, and recognized as such by the known world. St. Clair County, Illinois was now highly improved, and acknowledged one of the best counties in the state. It would compare favorably with an equal area of any state in the Union in the production of wheat, corn, and coal.

The Pacific Rail Road would take him to this place in five and a half days, but now Providence interfered. He now looked back to the days he stood on the banks of the Mississippi River, thirty-five long years ago; his determination then was to make a fortune. By 35 years of hard and diligent labor, he had accomplished this: he was now a rich man, his boyhood dreams were all realized, and now when he thought of enjoying it, he was stricken down by disease.

But this was only a forerunner of what was yet to come. It has often been stated that afflictions never come alone. It proved so in Mr. A.'s case. His cup of woe was yet to be filled to the brim before he was to be called away from his earthly home. The reader can imagine how hard it was to give up the long cherished hope of ever again seeing his early home–"but what can't be cured must be endured,"–so he had to make the best of it.

His mind was not impaired by the stroke, and he was able to ride around in a buggy by having a driver; his daughter Caroline, now budding into womanhood, would hitch up a horse and drive for him. He was thus enabled to oversee his business by having some one to talk for him, as he was only able to talk in monosyllables, being able to say yes, no, and a few other short words. His physician informed him that he was liable to have another attack at any moment; he was aware of this, and concluded to have his business all settled and straightened up, and have every thing on a sure footing. He drew up his will, and divided his property among his heirs as he thought best; he showed no partiality, but tried to divide as nearly equal as he could.

The personal property he still kept in his possession, as he still continued to buy and sell, loan money, etc. He, with the aid of a cane, was enabled to walk around about the house, to go from room to room, and in this manner he passed the rest of his days. He was Cyrus Alexander still, but not the Cyrus Alexander any more who knew no fear, nor never flinched to face the largest Grizzly bear that California could scare up.

Alexander held considerable property in and around Healdsburg. In Healdsburg he held a mortgage on the Academy; this institution was built and owned by a Mr. Scott. It struggled hard to get along, but the country did not give it the patronage that it deserved and was worthy of, and it failed. Mr. A. gave the parties a fair chance and a good show, but as it kept increasing in debt, and the indebtness ran into the thousands, Mr. A. closed the mortgage. He now owned the Academy and had no use for it. It is situated in a nice and desirable part of the town; he could have divided the property and sold the lots, and got his money back;

he could easily have done this, or let it remain as it was, and increase in value, as the town was fast building up. But such was not his intention; he did not look at it in that light; his sole object was not to make money, or to try and make a big thing out of the Academy.

The building had been put up for a High School, the town and surrounding country needed such an institution, and he was determined that it should remain as such. He looked about for some one to take charge of it and make it answer its legitimate purpose; no one seeming to care about running the risk, he concluded he would present it to some religious society, and see what they could do with it.

It had been tried as a private enterprise and failed; he thought perhaps a denominational institution would be better. So he presented it to the Presbyterian Church, giving them a good deed for it, thus placing it out of debt and on a solid and sure foundation, and ready for work.

The Presbyterians went to work to fit it up for use; they elected a board of trustees to arrange things. The trustees named the institution *Alexander Academy*, in honor of the donor. By this you see that the Rocky Mountain trapper actually became the founder of an institution of learning. At the present time, the Institution is under the supervision of Mr. R. McCulloch, he having leased it for a term of five years, three of which have expired, leaving him two years yet to run. We have not visited the school personally, but judging from what we hear of it, it is doing pretty well, but might do much better. Some people however think that their children can learn better when they go to the expense of sending them away from home.

Mr. A., having more grapes than he used for his family, thought he would turn the surplus amount into wine, so that he could treat his neighbors and friends when they came to see him. But he soon found that it made some of the boys in the neighborhood feel and act rather funny; he made the following remark—"it might do for vinegar, but it was poor stuff for boys"—and from this time he made no more wine. He perhaps saw that "Wine is a mocker and strong drink raging."

One thing in particular that we wish to remark here is this: Alexander, although he was generous and never called stingy, was very particular never to waste anything wilfully. "Young America" of today is just the opposite of this; you will find the rising generation very careless and wasteful, some thinking it unnecessary to save unless they can save in large quantities and as they never get hold of the large quantities, they never save anything, and drift along without any definite object in view, and perhaps never have a home of their own.

Mr. A. must have habituated himself to this by saving his ammunition while in the Mountains, and the habit always clung to him during life. We have watched him while loading his rifle, he was very careful not to waste even a single grain of powder, or in cutting the bullet patch, how very careful he would be that nothing should be lost. Another thing that may have taught Mr. A. this very important habit perhaps was that he was thrown on his own resources; he had no indulgent father with him to help him along and pay his bills for him; he had to hoe his own row, and if he did not care, he alone would suffer the consequences.

This habit alone brought thousands of dollars to his coffers during his lifetime. It is no difficult thing to earn a dollar, but quite a task to save one. Earning money and saving money are two different things, as many a poor chap can tell to his sorrow. Some perhaps think that Mr. A. became wealthy because he was a lucky man, but had he squandered as fast as he earned, he would never have saved anything. We doubt if *luck* had anything at all to do with it.

After the close of the late Civil War, many noticed how reckless and careless the returning soldiers were. They had been where every thing had been carried on with a high hand; Uncle Sam has to pay for it, so what is the difference! They saw destruction and waste on every hand, and this wastefulness became a habit with them; it seemed natural that they should be wasteful, and this habit still clings to some of them, and will cling to many a poor chap all of his life. Their every action shows it.

The reader is aware that when Mr. A. crossed the Gulf, he lost his all; thus he entered California without a dollar, and only one poor, torn, worn suit of clothes. At the end of this volume we will give the value of his wealth when he died.[1] He did not possess a dollar; he was away from home with no one to depend upon but himself; no one to care if he lived or died. He toiled and saved, and success crowned him at last. If any one ever practiced true economy, Cyrus Alexander did.

The immortal Webster said: "adversity and opposition will make a man when all other means fail." Perhaps this was the case with our hero, as he had enough of both to contend with. For years, opposition faced him at every move he made, and he and adversity were no strangers.

Strangers were inclined to think that Mr. A. was cold and stern and unsocial, simply because he was naturally still; he never had much to say, not even in carrying on his business. At his own house he would prefer to listen to others rather than talk himself. On asking him if he was always this way he replied that he must have acquired the habit while out in the mountains with his two companions, there being no chance for a variety of subjects, and those of common interest became worn and threadbare; they received no news, and soon tired of telling their hopes and ex-

[1] The author apparently intended to do so, but there is a blank space after the words: "Mr. Alexander died worth . . ." in Chapter 9.

pectations. Mr. A. said they would sit around their campfire in the evening for hours at a time without saying a word, seeming to prefer silence. So when in company, he seemed to think it his place to listen. But when questioned, he was ever ready with an answer, particularly if it related to mountaineering, or to any of the early settlers of this state. All seemed to be acquainted with each other, from San Diego to Mount Shasta and Humboldt Bay. Alexander was never a proud man, but as he was an "Old Californian," it seemed proper that he should be questioned. All new comers were inclined to ask a great many questions, and as he had been here so long and had seen so much of pioneer life, he thought it was his place to answer all civil questions; this too helped to make him incommunicative.

Any one coming to his door, poor, starving, or in need of help, always found a willing and ready friend in Uncle Cyrus. He never turned any one away hungry or empty handed. "He had been there" himself, and knew just what it was to be without a dollar or a friend in this cold wide world.

Mr. Alexander tried all known means to regain his health, but all to no purpose; he visited and tried the different mineral Springs; placed himself under the treatment of the best and most skillful of Physicians, but it was not so to be. Old age was creeping on, and he could feel that his sands of life were nearly run; he was fast fading away. Camp and Mountain life had brought health and vigor to him in his early days, but he had followed it too long; his exposure and hard manual labor began to leave its traces on him.

About a year after his first stroke of Paralysis, he received another; this second stroke was a very severe one. This kept him confined to his house for a long time; his friends tried to rally him up, but he was now very weak. He recovered sufficiently to be around some again, but he was now a weak and feeble old man.

About this time, a severe trial was demanded of him; as he was fast passing away, he began to count on his son William to manage his business affairs for him, and should the worst happen, William was to fill his place as much as possible. Several of his children were quite small and needed a father's care; he had trained William in the way he should go. William had been in the milling business; here the seeds of that most dreaded disease, Consumption, were sown; William's health began to fail, and Mr. A., becoming alarmed about him, concluded to send him to sea. He first tried medical skill, change of climate, mineral springs, etc., but received no benefit from them. So William started on his sea voyage to the Sandwich Islands. All bade William good-bye and wished him success in the restoration of his health. But it was the last time that they ever saw William.

The rough ocean voyage was too much for his delicate constitution, and on the 16th of August 1867, he died aged 21 years 11 months and 15 days. His destination was Honolulu, but he died before he reached his destination, and his body was committed to the waves, and he found a watery grave. The news of William's death brought mourning into the family. Alexander grieved sorely over the death of his first born. William was a good boy, but his death was not altogether unexpected. He had been sent to sea as a last resource. Alexander's friends sympathized with him in this his great grief, and he submitted with Christian fortitude.

Alexander, after becoming able to go about again, looked after his business affairs, but business was kept quiet, we might say almost in a dormant state for some time, until the marriage of his daughter to William M. Mulligan,[2] when his son-in-law conducted his business affairs.

He now sent his second son Henry to school to prepare him for the business world. Henry was a stout, healthy boy, and went to work in earnest trying to obtain an education. He pored over his books, and took but little out door exercise; this proved fatal to him. He came home to recruit his health and to recover from what he considered a severe cold. But alas! instead of getting better, he constantly grew worse. They procured the best medical aid for him, but as

[2] William Mulligan was born in Glasgow, Missouri, July 23, 1838. He came to California in 1862. On July 30, 1868, he married Margaret, eldest daughter of Cyrus Alexander.

he constantly grew worse and Quick Consumption set in Alexander saw that he, too, must die. Henry continued to get worse until July 9th, 1869, when death relieved him from his sufferings. Henry was aged 17 years and 14 days.

This was another heavy blow for Mr. Alexander. He had now been deprived of his two oldest sons, both young men grown. He was now old and feeble, and saw that earth was not going to claim him much longer. He had hoped to live long enough to see his business controlled by one of his oldest sons. And as they both died so near together it made his afflictions still more severe. Hard as providence seemed to deal with him, he was never heard to complain or murmur. If his sympathizing friends spoke of his great loss, he would answer as well as he could articulate, "It seems hard but we are born to trouble." He was now confined to his house most of the time; he would occasionally take a ride by being helped into his buggy. Also now and then [he went to] visit a friend. There is an old adage which says: "As long as there is life, there is hope." Alexander thought so; he still visited many of the Springs noted for their medicinal qualities in hopes of finding some relief. He bathed in the mineral waters; others had received relief, and why should not he? But Providence had ordained otherwise, and health was never again to be restored to him.

After his second stroke, he was deprived of the power of reading; this was a great privation to him. He had spent much of his time of late years in reading, and now this great comfort was denied him. He had of late taken much interest in the doings of the world, the new inventions springing up almost every day, the new and improved machinery, the settlement of his adopted state, education, politics, religion, etc.

The newspapers were perused carefully and closely by him; he read many books; he enjoyed reading, as he had been for years without any reading matter whatever, but now this was denied him. He now had to depend upon others to read to him. He had always been a good man; he had dealt honorably with his fellow men and they did not desert him in this his great affliction. They often called on him and would read to him by the hour; he enjoyed all visits, and treated his visitors in such a manner that they as well as he enjoyed the visit.

CHAPTER IX.

Politics and Religion

IN POLITICS Alexander was a Republican. When the Republican Party agitated the Slave question and were in favor of freeing the slaves, Mr. A. sided with them. He was in favor of freedom and advocated the cause of freedom. While out among the Mountains, and in leading the early pioneer life of California he lost the run of politics, and in this way lost some of the interest he would otherwise have manifested. He never picked up the political tide as many others have done who were similarly situated; he had no hankering for office, nor did he ever seek political honor; he was content with the life he was leading. The last vote he cast was for Booth as Governor of California.[1] His friends aided him to get to the Polls, and kept him posted in the politics of the day; he was ever ready and willing to cast his vote, and considered the power of voting a sacred trust.

[1] Newton Booth (1825-1892) was elected state senator in 1863, governor in 1871, and United States senator in 1875.

In religion he was thoroughly Calvinistic. By the advice of Rev. A. L. S. Bateman, he became a member of the Presbyterian Church, and while a member of that church led a consistent Christian life. He filled the office of Deacon for several years. In his habits he was very temperate, in eating as well as in drinking. The Barrooms and Gambling Hells had no attraction for him. California in her early days held out many temptations and inducements, but Mr. A. avoided them all. The wild frolicking hurdy-gurdy life that many of his early associates led did not cause him once to think of following their example. His early training told him it was a vicious life, and that was enough for him. We think we can safely say that no one ever saw him enter a saloon and take a drink at the bar. And he did not keep any intoxicating liquor at home. He used tobacco, but in a mild form; he smoked the California Cigarita, and chewed some in middle life. But he was so careful that a stranger would hardly detect that he used tobacco at all. After he was stricken down with disease, he found that tobacco was an injury to him, so he quit the use of the weed altogether.

In his early part of California life, he was very careless about keeping the Sabbath. But it was the custom of the country to drive stock or ride off on business on that day. In speaking of this at one time he said he was sorry such was the case, but he did not see how he could remedy it; if he did not *rodeo* his stock on Sunday, he would not be able to get help. He preferred to rest on that day; he believed it was right to keep the Sabbath day holy, but it was customary to *rodeo* on Sunday, and he could not drive up his cattle alone and brand them.

Sunday at best is not regarded as a day of rest in the pioneer days of a new state. But time changes every thing, and time changes this. Alexander had higher hopes than mere earthly hopes. He did not altogether depend upon this earth for his happiness; he had faith in the world yet to come. He never said much on this or any other religious subject, but sometimes actions speak louder than words. During his last sickness, he took a great delight in having the Scriptures read to him. He was also fond of hearing people talking on religious subjects.

His religious opinion underwent a sudden change. He went to Healdsburg, stopped at the house of a friend, and sent for the Methodist minister, Rev. J. B. Fish, and united with that branch of the church. As he was not able to converse much, his friends never found out why he desired to change churches. But he seemed to understand and know what he was doing. He was highly pleased whenever a Minister would call on him. He afterwards had the Circuit Rider, Rev. G. McRea, to preach at his house, as he was not able to attend church. The preaching at his house continued almost up to his death.

Notwithstanding Alexander's poor health in early

manhood, and the hardships and dangers of a hard working, struggling, and adventurous life, he lived to a good old age. He outlived all his early associates in business, so far as we are aware of. White Cotton was killed by the Black Feet Indians in the Mountains; another of his chums was drowned while trying to cross the Gulf; and Capt. Fitch died at his residence at San Diego in 1849. And Alexander was called away from this world of strife, pain, and trouble on the 27th of December 1872, aged 67 years, 7 months, and 12 days. Peace to his ashes.

A large concourse of relatives and friends followed his mortal remains to its last resting place in the family graveyard near the house. The cemetery is situated on a beautiful knoll near the house. The two monuments and the head-stones can be seen from the road leading through the valley. A costly and beautiful monument is erected over Mr. Alexander's grave. A monument also marks the resting place of William and Henry.

The Cemetery contains the following named members of Alexander's family. It will be seen that Providence claimed much of him, as the dead outnumber the living.

JANE died May 10th, 1852.
Aged 1 year, 10 months and 8 days.

ELLEN died June 28th, 1856.
Aged 7 years, 10 months and 16 days.

ALBERT died March 12th, 1858.
Aged 1 year, 6 months and 27 days.

WILLIAM died August 16th, 1867.
Aged 21 years, 11 months and 13 days.

HENRY died July 7th, 1869.
Aged 17 years and 14 days.

CYRUS died December 27th, 1872.
Aged 67 years, 7 months and 12 days.

Besides these, it contains two of his children who died in infancy.

Alexander lived long enough to see all his boyhood dreams realized. He made a fortune, became very rich, and then died, just as he was having things arranged so that he could enjoy life. How many others meet the same fate.

Mr. Alexander died worth.... He lived long enough to see his third son Joseph old enough to conduct business. It was a great satisfaction to him in his declining years to see that Joe was industrious and persevering. Joseph was married to Miss Kate Turner on the 27th of October 1874. He has a ranch and is living near the old homestead, and is engaged in sheep raising.

Alexander finished the house he had started in 1847 in good style. It is two stories high; the upper story is frame; the house is painted white; the building is porched on two sides. It is yet (1876) the largest house in Alexander Valley, and is elegantly and expensively furnished, and furnished with the best of furniture. Mrs. Cyrus Alexander, with three of her children, Caroline, aged . . . ,[2] Thomas 12, and George 7 years old, occupy the home place. Margaret and her husband live near the homestead. While writing up this book, we have had occasion many times to call on Mrs. Alexander. Every thing is quiet there now, and no one in now visiting the place could form an idea of the stir and bustle that was formerly carried on there.

The place is nicely fitted up; the house is surrounded with a nice yard containing shade trees and many varieties of flowers, which grow so luxuriantly in this mild climate. All necessary barns, stables, smoke-house, granaries, etc., are built of the best material, and in late designs. Mrs. Alexander still keeps stirring around, always busy, and never contented unless at work. She does not go out very much, but seems pleased when every one calls on her. She never tires of speaking of her husband. She is proud of having the honor of being the wife of Cyrus Alexander. She is trying to educate her children. She is a kind and indulgent mother, and has the respect and esteem of all her neighbors and acquaintances.

One thing to be regretted about her is this: she never learned to speak the English language very fluently, and unless a person is well acquainted with her and has some knowledge of the Spanish language

[2] The age is omitted in the manuscript. She was born March 17, 1860.

he will not be able to understand much of what she says. She generally manages to have one of her children with her to interpret for her. She is still young looking to be the mother of so many children. And none in meeting her would think she had been a Pioneer's wife. She is under medium height, heavy set, dark complexion, quick of movement, and very industrious; she is forty-five years of age, but looks much younger. She has good health, and the chances are in her favor for a long life.

Conclusion

ADVICE TO "YOUNG AMERICA."

Had Alexander been elected to fill public offices, had he served as Governor or Senator, his name would have been heralded throughout the land. He would then have been called publicly a *great man*. But today, should many of our so called great men who are now slumbering with the silent dead arise, look around them, see what laudable remarks the papers have been making about them, and then read the epitaph on their tombstones, they would evidently think they were occupying the wrong graves.

Our country is very generous, ever ready to praise and applaud. If any man occupying public office should make some remark that time, by chance, might verify, at once he is petted as a man that possesses more than the ordinary run of intelligence; if not considered a prophet, he would be considered a seer.

Good and *Bad* men are less so than they seem. But when a man devotes a life-time in farming, roughing out a pioneer's life, assists others in getting a home in the wilds, braves the danger of Indians and wild animals, helps pioneer schools, churches, and charitable institutions, does all in his power to help a new Territory or state, nothing is said of him. Alexander was a great man, even if he was not an officer, statesman, or politician. He was a great man in his way. He professed to be an agricultural man, an independent farmer, and he fulfilled his station. He helped to open up and civilize the proud and haughty state of California.

He began life in California without a dollar, and never did possess a dollar but what he worked for or came by honestly. When a boy, he had but one object in view; he wanted to be a rich man; he did not care for greatness; he did not wish to be supported by the government; he simply wanted to make a fortune. He kept this one thing in view; it occupied much of his time; it haunted him in his dreams, and he pressed on until his object was gained.

While young, he never considered himself above work, but showed a willingness to learn any thing that came along; in this manner he became possessed of knowledge which proved worth almost a fortune to him in after life. Another peculiar thing about this man: he never stopped to murmur or complain when misfortunes overtook him, but always trusted in the future and went on with renewed energy.

Great fortitude was required in leaving his home and friends to seek a fortune in the "Western Wilds"; gold was then unknown, and consequently did not lure him out here as it did thousands of others; great energy and perseverance were necessary in order to get that fortune when once beyond civilization. He tried one thing after another until he struck the right trail. He would have remained a Rocky Mountain hunter several years more than he did had the Black Feet Indians left him alone, but he saw that they had the power, and that they were not backward in using it. His business pursuits at San Diego would not have amounted to much in the long run. He hit the nail on the head when he became a land owner in California. But even this would not have benefitted him much during life, had not gold been accidentally discovered.

He was an honest man, and considered so by all with whom he had business connections. He was ever ready to lend a helping hand to the poor and afflicted, ever ready to aid, and give his influence in favor of education, religion, civilization, and always stood up for Uncle Sam.

Now in conclusion, if the reader has been benefitted one single iota; if one new idea has been gained; if it has caused a new determination; if grit, gumption, pluck, and perseverance will be kept in view; our object has been gained.

BIBLIOGRAPHY

Altrocchi, Julia Cooley. *The Old California Trail.* Caldwell, Idaho, 1945.

Bancroft, Hubert Howe. *History of California.* Vol. 2, p. 689; vol. 3, pp. 388, 408; vol. 4, pp. 117, 583.

Bancroft, Hubert Howe. *Register of Pioneer Inhabitants of California 1542 to 1848.* Los Angeles, Dawson's Book Shop, 1964.

Barrett, Samuel A. *The Ethno-geography of the Pomo and Neighboring Indians.* University of California Publications in American Archaeology and Ethnology, VI. University of California Press.

Caughey, John Walton. *California.* Englewood Cliffs, New Jersey (1964).

Cleland, Robert Glass. *This Reckless Breed of Men.* New York, 1950.

Cowan, Robert G. *Ranchos of California.* Fresno, 1956.

Finley, Ernest Latimar, ed. *History of Sonoma County.* Santa Rosa, Press Democrat Publishing Co., 1937, pp. 182, 187, 238, 292.

Fitch, Mrs. Henry D. (Josefa Carrillo de Fitch.) "Narracion." Manuscript in the Bancroft Library.

Fremont, John C. *Narratives of Exploration and Adventure.* New York, 1956.

Gregory, Tom. *History of Sonoma County, California.* Los Angeles, Historical Record Co., 1911, pp. 792-94.

Gudde, Erwin G. *California Place Names.* Berkeley, 1965.

Hansen, Harvey J. & Miller, Jean Thurlow. *Wild Oats in Eden.* Santa Rosa, 1962.

Hoover, Mildred Brooke; Rensch, Hero Eugene; & Rensch, Ethel Grace. *Historic Spots in California.* Stanford (1964).

Howard, Robert West. *The Great Iron Trail.* New York (1962).

Illustrated History of Sonoma County. Chicago, Lewis Publishing Co., 1889, pp. 265-66.

Langhart, Edwin. Letter, August 24, 1965.

Menefee, C. A. *Historical and Descriptive Sketch Book of Napa, Sonoma, Lake and Mendocino.* Napa City, Reporter Publishing House, 1873.

Munro-Fraser, J. P., ed. *History of Sonoma County, California.* San Francisco, Alley, Bowen and Co., 1880, pp. 50, 60, 212-17, 239-40, 354-58.

New Historical Atlas of Sonoma County, California. Oakland, Thomas H. Thompson and Co., 1877, p. 92.

Paul, Rodman W. *California Gold.* Lincoln, Nebraska, 1947.

Pomeroy, Earl. *The Pacific Slope.* New York, 1965.

Templeton, Sardis W. *The Lame Captain.* Los Angeles, 1965.

Tuomey, Honoria. *History of Sonoma County.* Chicago, S. J. Clarke Publishing Co., 1926, vol. 1, pp. 250, 251, 388, 422-23.

Wilkes, Captain Charles. *Narrative of the United States Exploring Expedition.* 5 vols. Philadelphia, 1844.

Woods, Rev. James A. *Recollections of Pioneer Work in California.* San Francisco, 1878.

INDEX